THE DUOGENIC LEADER

THE DUOGENIC LEADER

*Unlock Your Endogenic
and Exogenic Power*

Beatrice Aebi-Magee, PhD

EDITED BY JOHN AEBI-MAGEE

AEBI SYSTEMS LLC

Edited by John Aebi-Magee

Published by
Aebi Systems LLC
Lake Oswego, Oregon, USA
To contact the author or publisher visit:
www.aebisystems.com

® Duogenic, Endogenic, and Exogenic are registered trademarks of Beatrice Aebi-Magee, PhD.

This publication is sold with the understanding that the author and publisher are not engaged in rendering counseling or other clinical services. If counseling advice is required, the services of a competent professional should be sought out.

First Edition, 2013

Library of Congress Control Number: 2013938707

ISBN: 978-0989335300

Aebi Systems

www.aebisystems.com

The states of Endogenic and Exogenic lead you on characteristically different paths. These two paths produce different outcomes, and over time, they result in profoundly different life stories

CONTENTS

PREFACE

I felt driven to write this book because I could see the tremendous benefit psychology brings to the business world. Very few business leaders also have decades of psychological study. If more leaders can comprehend the human psyche, they can guide others and assist their companies, divisions, departments, and groups to overcome dysfunctional human dynamics, destructive interactional patterns, and self-created complications. Leaders are ideally positioned to be role models because people implicitly expect that leaders know better.

Work can be a place where you are challenged, stimulated, inspired, and where you prosper and grow with others as you reach ambitious shared goals and horizons. When people use their energy for overcoming challenges and making progress, work becomes a greater place to be and to learn from one another.

Why not make communication easy instead of complicated, resolve conflicts instead of build walls, prevent a crisis instead of live in crisis mode, or find clarity instead of stay confused? We can create workplaces that are sizzling with the promise of growth, creativity, productivity, curiosity, fun, joy, and strategic relentlessness in human growth, prosperity, and discovery.

The concept of Duogenic power provides a simple, uncompromised approach for tapping into the essence of what the greatest schools of psychology since Freud have brought forth. Drawing from my studies in humanistic, existential, cognitive, behavioral, body-centered, gestalt, neuropsychology, and deep psychology, and from my practice as a Swiss psychoanalyst and leadership consultant, I have found that all tools for healing, personal growth, and personal power have one common denominator: they build Endogenic reliance, Exogenic reliance, or both.

For over two decades, I have applied the principles described in this book through my work with corporate executives and business leaders. Together, we solved problematic demands and tough challenges related to leadership advancement, innovation, and strategic decisions. Through the lens of Endogenic and Exogenic, business leaders more easily find clarity. Living with greater clarity frees up energy and time, individually and collectively, and allows for healthier, faster advancement of business and society, all with more joyful stamina.

May 2013
Beatrice Aebi-Magee, PhD

PART ONE:

TWO STATES OF

BEING

CHAPTER ONE

A FUNDAMENTAL PRINCIPLE

The best leaders have developed the freedom to choose between Endogenic and Exogenic and do not automatically overuse their Exogenic state

There are exactly two ways to experience any given moment: in the Endogenic state or the Exogenic state. This simplified fundamental principle of human psychology is, for the first time, presented in this book.

Every moment holds a myriad of possibilities. What you do, think, sense, or feel will be different depending on if you are in the Endogenic or Exogenic state at that instant. Simply choosing between Endogenic and Exogenic multiplies your chances for making the most out of every moment in life.

You are invited to freely explore a new way of looking at yourself and others. Your ability for discerning behaviors, interactions, and human dynamics will grow as you learn more about yourself, connect better with others, and have greater impact and effectiveness in all aspects of life.

Understanding the distinction between Endogenic and Exogenic provides a simple and powerful tool for rapidly advancing maturity, intelligence, and wisdom. It can immediately help you become a more powerful leader, unlock your innovative potential, better understand others, solve complex problems faster, have less confusion and greater clarity in life, quickly advance your intelligence, improve your relationships with others, become a better parent, advance your career faster, become physically more healthy, prevent dysfunctional behavior, strengthen your stamina, have more joy in living, and lead a more fulfilling life. It is an avenue for advancing personal power.

The words Endogenic and Exogenic represent the opposing nature of our two states of mind. One state arises from within the moment, where what we think and do emerges from what we sense and feel. The other state is linked to the past or future, where our thoughts, feelings, and actions are determined by memories, knowledge, and experiences. One state excludes the other at every given moment.

Everything you think, feel, and do always occurs when you are in one state or the other. Depending on which state you are in, Endogenic or Exogenic, you feel differently, think differently, and act differently—and you are experienced differently by others. Over years, these differences shape your character traits and your path in life.

Learning about the Endogenic and Exogenic states reveals patterns, strengths, and weaknesses in yourself and others and provides insight into what drives success.

You can learn what state you are in and you can choose the one that is better suited for any given instant. To maximize intelligence, leadership, and success, you must balance your reliance on both states.

The principle of Endogenic and Exogenic is recognizable by everyone. We sense the difference. By naming and describing these states, it becomes possible to see the world through a lens that can be applied to every form of human thought, action, and feeling.

Society trains us to favor our Exogenic state and override our Endogenic state, so most people do not know how to draw on both states purposely or how to instantly choose one over the other. Much of what we call good luck is the result of being in the right state at the crucial time, and most of the confusion we experience in life is merely a result of being in the wrong state for what the situation or instant demands.

Self-limitations are caused by unknowingly being in the wrong state. Not knowing which state we are in or how each state will impact a given situation puts us at a disadvantage. We end up ineffective or limited. We complicate and confuse things. When you learn to use both states, you quickly overcome many self-limitations.

Whether you rely fully on your Endogenic and Exogenic states and whether you have the freedom to choose between the two determines your strength as a leader. The best leaders have developed the freedom to choose between Endogenic and Exogenic and do not automatically overuse their Exogenic state.

If you are like most people who want to be successful in life, you have worked hard acquiring the knowledge, experience, and credentials that allow you to advance and flourish. As you draw from memories, knowledge, and experience, you form opinions, analyze data, meet expectations, stay on task, focus on goals, follow directions, and anticipate results. You can define yourself by your status, ideals, wealth, title, resume, and history, and by the people you associate with.

These are all Exogenic qualities. Taken to an extreme, and when not balanced with Endogenic reliance, they rob us of satisfaction and fulfillment in life. When Exogenic qualities are overvalued and over dominant, we find less meaning in life and gradually lose our ability for creativity, innovation, sensing, and feeling. Only in the Endogenic state can you be creative, original, and genuine. The Endogenic state is not planned. It is completely real and true to the moment.

The purpose of *The Duogenic Leader* is to reveal the power that you gain through strengthening and balancing your Endogenic and Exogenic states. With strength and balance, you open a realm of possibilities in life. You can drastically increase your accuracy in predicting outcomes, driving results, reading reactions in others, and being attentive to detail while not losing sight of the whole.

When you understand Endogenic and Exogenic in yourself and others, you will make better decisions, communicate more easily, reduce your blind spots, and have greater influence on issues you are passionate about. You will discover that people want to follow your lead because of who you are.

With strong and balanced Endogenic and Exogenic states, business leaders experience a competitive advantage through an increase in personal strength, being able to resolve challenges faster, acting with greater clarity, anticipating changes before others do, understanding themselves and others better, gaining deep personal respect from coworkers, leading people more confidently, and accelerating their own growth. Having access to both the Endogenic state and Exogenic state allows a leader to have influential strength and provides agility and ease to be more strategic, proactive, creative, compassionate, and insightful.

At every moment, whether you are relaxing or facing a challenge, you are either in your Endogenic state or in your Exogenic state. If you do not choose the state, you will be in your default state. We continue forward in life as though there were no choice about which state we are in or which state is best to be in. You will gain power when you begin to question your default state and learn to choose which state you want to be in.

The concept of Endogenic and Exogenic needs to be experienced. The only way to comprehend it is by discovering your own Endogenic state and experiencing what happens when you choose one state over the other.

CHAPTER TWO

ENDOGENIC

We are only in the Endogenic state as long as we sense and feel the present moment

The Endogenic state is the psychological state of mind where everything we think, feel, or do is connected to the present moment. In that moment, your thoughts, feelings, and actions become spontaneously known to you.

The word Endogenic is derived from the Greek words endon "within" and -genes "born." What we think and do emerges from what we sense and feel. In the Endogenic state, we have an extreme heightened sense of awareness and performance. We have no attachment to a memory, expectation, belief, goal, concept, label, or other reference to the past or future. Everything is new, as though it had not been done, thought, or felt the same way before. We do not compare, scrutinize, analyze, or judge. We are not running on autopilot or behaving as conditioned. We are not tied to what we have learned.

In the Endogenic state, your thoughts and actions are creative, original, and genuine. We connect with others, listen receptively, and are responsive, compassionate, and empathetic. In the Endogenic state, we are in touch with others and with our environment. We easily make connections among previously unrelated notions. There is no false persona and nothing artificial about a person in the Endogenic state. Our status, title, resume, and history are all irrelevant to us in that moment. We are flexible and resourceful and do not need to have all the answers.

For most people, the very idea of switching to the Endogenic state sounds impossible. We have been trained and conditioned to prefer our Exogenic state. To enter the Endogenic state, we must slow down, relax, and let go of demands. We must turn toward an inner focus in the present moment to experience our thoughts, feelings, sensations, and behaviors. Time seems to slow down. We may experience the Endogenic state for a fraction of a second or minutes or hours.

Everyone has experienced their Endogenic state. The more profound experiences include feeling love, having a moment of inspiration, engaging in a meaningful and deep conversation, suddenly understanding a complex situation with an aha moment, feeling at one with nature, or truly inspiring another person. The abilities to invent, create, induce, experience, inspire, gauge, improvise, have intuition, or make discoveries are Endogenic. Every discovery that was ever made came from the Endogenic state. Having a sense of wonder about the world is driven by the curiosity of the Endogenic state. Only in the Endogenic state can a person see something and be in awe or curious or enchanted. The ability to find meaning and to trust your resourcefulness is also Endogenic.

The Endogenic state always ends by switching to the Exogenic state. We are only in the Endogenic state as long as we sense and feel the present moment. As soon as we are directed by a memory, expectation, belief, goal, concept, definition, or other reference to the past or future, we have left the Endogenic state.

Endogenic:

the psychological state during which your sensations, feelings, thoughts, and behavior are uniquely generated as an expression of being in the present moment. In the Endogenic state, feelings arise spontaneously and thought and behavior emerges from what you sense and feel. [antonym: Exogenic]

CHAPTER THREE

EXOGENIC

For most adults, the Exogenic state is what we are most familiar with.
We have been trained and conditioned to prefer our Exogenic state

The Exogenic state is the psychological state of mind where everything we think, feel, or do is linked to the past or future. You draw from memories, knowledge, and experience to form opinions, analyze data, meet expectations, stay on task, focus on goals, follow directions, and anticipate results.

The word Exogenic is derived from the Greek words exo "outside" and -genes "born." What we think, feel, and do is linked to an ultimate reference point outside of the present moment. For most adults, the Exogenic state is what we are most familiar with. We have been trained and conditioned to prefer our Exogenic state. In the Exogenic state, we depend on the world around us and we trust what we have learned. We apply our experience and knowledge to survive, to function as part of society, and to acquire what we want in life.

A musician can replicate an orchestral piece through the precision and outward focus of the Exogenic state. Every note must exactly match a previously determined pattern. Most of the human-made things you see around you were produced by people working in the Exogenic state by carefully following set procedures and repetitive tasks. In the Exogenic state, we have goal oriented drive and determination. We can excel at almost anything through hard work, repetition, and memorization—even when talent or passion is not evident. Rather than discover something new, in the Exogenic state, we efficiently repeat what we already know or copy what someone else knows. In the Exogenic state, everything we think, feel, or do builds from what has been thought, felt, or done before.

The Exogenic state allows us to control our pace. Thoughts, feelings, and actions can occur rapidly without need for reflection or contemplation. Time easily becomes an enemy, so when we work toward a goal, we have little patience for emotions, diversions, or unexpected playful behavior. In the Exogenic state, we are not bound by what the moment holds and we can ignore what is going on around us. We may not even notice some of our own actions or expressions.

In the Exogenic state, feelings are thought not sensed. Instead of feeling an emotion, we think of an emotion or recall a feeling from a previous occurrence and then we believe we feel it. Only in the Endogenic state can you feel an emotion that has not been self-fabricated.

The Exogenic state allows us to alter our own attitude. We can decide to be happy, be positive, stay focused, or be alert. We create a persona that can mislead others and we can cover up our insecurities. We can smile when we are not happy, say yes when we mean no, and figure out how to look better than those around us. We can behave brave when we are frightened. We define ourselves by our status, ideals, wealth, title, resume, history, and whom we associate with. We are able to adapt to diverse social settings and fit in. In the Exogenic state, we are able to speak with authority, give clear instructions, and appear to be an expert. Words prevail over senses and emotions. We talk to others without feeling empathy, and we strive to have all the answers.

The seduction of the Exogenic state is speed and predictability. This creates a sense of security, but brings with it a risk of losing accuracy, stifling innovation, and losing meaning in life. The only way to leave the Exogenic state is to switch to the Endogenic state. This occurs constantly throughout the day. The greater our fear and insecurity, the more we become dependent on being in the Exogenic state.

Exogenic:

the psychological state during which feelings are thought not sensed, and thoughts and behavior are products of memories, knowledge, beliefs, goals, expectations, or rules generated outside the present moment. In the Exogenic state, you feel how you believe, thoughts are replicated, and behavior is independent of what you feel. [antonym: Endogenic]

CHAPTER FOUR

DUOGENIC

You can quickly overcome many self-limitations when you learn to use both states at will

A Duogenic leader has learned to strengthen and balance the Endogenic and Exogenic states and has discovered the ability to consciously choose which state is most appropriate for any given moment. Strength, balance, and awareness of choice are the most important factors for developing Duogenic leadership.

When we face a difficult decision, challenge, problem, or conflict, it is possible to choose to address it in the Endogenic state or the Exogenic state. When we do not choose, we react in our default state, which for most people is Exogenic. For example, we often say what is appropriate or expected instead of what we sense or feel. Responding to meet expectations occurs when we are in the Exogenic state and expressing what we sense or feel in the moment occurs in the Endogenic state. By choosing the Endogenic state, you will often surprise or inspire others with your accuracy and honesty. By choosing the Exogenic state, you can prepare your actions and meet expectations. If you do not choose between the two, you respond in your default state and your power as a leader is diminished.

Society has developed a destructive bias in favor of the Exogenic state. Through parenting, education, role models at work, and mutual support, we continuously strengthen our Exogenic state and minimize our Endogenic state. This process begins in childhood and gradually takes over our lives, robbing us of intelligence, meaning, fulfillment, and joy. We suffer from the loss as individuals and as a society.

All self-limitations are caused by being unknowingly in the wrong state. Not knowing which state we are in or how each state will impact a given situation puts us at a disadvantage. We end up ineffective or limited. We complicate and confuse things. You can quickly overcome many self-limitations when you learn to use both states at will.

The ability to choose Endogenic or Exogenic takes introspection, contemplation, and observation of yourself and others. Once you recognize the distinction between Endogenic and Exogenic, you will see it clearly and constantly and you will discover the power in Duogenic leadership.

By developing strength and reliance on both your Endogenic and Exogenic states, you eliminate blind spots that jeopardize intelligent action and you break through barriers that limit your potential. By strengthening your Endogenic and Exogenic states and by learning how to choose between them, you experience continuous life-changing breakthroughs in intelligence and well-being.

CHAPTER FIVE

DICHOTOMIES

*People very commonly act from the wrong state, which makes their
actions ineffective*

Certain actions or outcomes require that we be in one state or the
other. If you want to be uniquely creative, you need to be in the
Endogenic state. If you observe someone following a recipe or
copying something, that person is in the Exogenic state. To
control you must be in your Exogenic state and to connect you
must be in your Endogenic state.

People very commonly act from the wrong state, which makes
their actions ineffective. For example, if you mean to take control
and direct a situation but are in the Endogenic state, your
gestures and tone of voice will instead signal connecting and
collaborative influence. You may wonder why you were not able
to direct others. On the other hand, if you feel like creatively
cooking and, being in the Endogenic state, start adding
ingredients as you please, you might not end up with the dish that
you promised someone.

It is helpful to think about dichotomies to understand the power
of each state. The following table shows samples of Endogenic-
Exogenic dichotomies.

Examples of Dichotomies	
Endogenic	Exogenic
Present	Past or future
Connecting	Controlling

Examples of Dichotomies	
Endogenic	**Exogenic**
Creative	Adaptive
Bottom-up	Top-down
Innovate	Replicate
Unique	Scalable
Original	Copy
New	Same
Discovery	Recipe
Unfold	Assemble
Fluid	Defining
Flowing	Mechanical
Spontaneous	Conditioned
Integrate	Separate
Experiential	Expectation
Perceiving	Judging
Comprehend	Memorize
Reflect	Distract
Process	Goal
Win-win	Compromise
Aware	Pay attention
Influence	Direct

Examples of Dichotomies	
Endogenic	Exogenic
Envision	Plan
Inspire	Instruct
Inherent life cycle	Desired duration
Curiosity	Belief
Unrestrained	Rules
Passion	Discipline
Accuracy	Precision
Engaging	Entitled
To be	To have
Contemplate	Presume
Synthesize	Analyze
Genuine	Appropriate
Ambiguous	Absolute
Unknown	Predictable

WHICH STATE AM I IN?

At any given moment, you are either in the Endogenic state or in the Exogenic state. By observing yourself and others, you will recognize this dichotomy. With the distinction comes an opportunity. You can stay in the state you are or choose the other. The table below illustrates examples for learning to differentiate between Endogenic and Exogenic.

Which State Am I In At This Moment?	
Endogenic	Exogenic
I am learning something new by experiencing it	I am learning something new by studying and memorizing it
I am looking forward to what this day brings	I hope I get this done by the deadline
I am creating something totally new	I am creating something by applying rules or copying what has been done before
I am approaching this change with discovery and curiosity	I am approaching this change by setting goals and making plans
I am seeking to engage and solicit others	I am seeking to control and direct others
I notice that I feel angry	I blow up when I'm in an argument
I start cleaning my desk because I feel in the mood	I clean my desk because it is on my checklist for today
I have an honest, meaningful and unpredictable conversation	I prepare for a conversation with notes and expectations

Which State Am I In At This Moment?	
Endogenic	Exogenic
I notice that I am not being heard	I keep talking and make my point
When my boss has a behavior I do not like, I speak with my boss about it.	I act friendly to a boss I dislike
I sense my friend needs help	I believe my friend when he says he is fine
I come up with a new way to manage a project	I follow project management procedures that worked before
I notice that my turn signal didn't turn off	My turn signal has been on for the last mile
I speak from my heart at a family gathering	I say what is expected at a family gathering
I face a personal crisis by comforting and caring for myself	I face a personal crisis by staying busy and forgetting the bad
I listen intently to an angry customer, show empathy for his frustration, and offer him options he will be delighted with	I respond to an angry customer by explaining to him how he is wrong
I am criticized and I understand what triggered the feedback	I am criticized and I immediately apologize
I feel unhappy	Life is good, I should be happy
I notice how my body feels at this moment	I do not realize it when my knee bounces rapidly
When my child does not want to put on a coat, we step outside to feel the cold	I make my child put on a warm coat before going outside

Which State Am I In At This Moment?	
Endogenic	Exogenic
I introduce two friends in a warm way and create a moment for them to connect	I quickly introduce two friends by mentioning each other's names and then continue on
I visit an art museum and wander until I feel drawn to a piece; I notice my reactions and stay there until I am done	I visit an art museum and notice when the pieces were painted, who painted them, and which ones I would want to own
I have 10 minutes before it is time to leave so I set my alarm, enjoy the peace and dare to lose myself	I have 10 minutes before it is time to leave so I get a few things done that are on my list
I look at the stars with wonder and amazement as I immerse myself in the experience of it	I look at the stars and try to spot the constellations I have learned

SEEING THE STATE OF OTHERS

You will have a strategic advantage as a leader if you learn to recognize whether other people are in their Endogenic or Exogenic states. This knowledge helps you more effectively interact with others, make quick and accurate decisions about people, and be confident about the trust you place in others. At any given moment, you will have greater insight about another person if you know what state the person is in.

To know what state others are in lets us see behind the stage. It opens a window of information. Once we differentiate what state a behavior comes from we can better understand the motivation that the behavior expresses.

A smile from someone in the Endogenic state is an expression of joy, love, or tenderness and the meaning is genuine. On the other hand, when someone who is in the Exogenic state smiles at you, the smile may signal friendliness but it is placed out of habit or premeditation. Similarly, when you hear an angry voice, if the person is in the Exogenic state it probably signals unrestrained frustration. However, coming from the Endogenic state, an angry voice is an expression of anger about what is going on at that moment, not from the day before or some unrelated reason.

When people want something from you, they are in the Exogenic state. Consider a sales person in a store who appears exceptionally friendly. If this person is in the Exogenic state, then the behavior is a means to the goal of making a sale. However, if the sales person is in the Endogenic state, that friendliness is not goal-oriented and comes from genuine interest in you or from a genuine pleasure in helping others.

At any given moment, you can only know what state others are in by first being in your Endogenic state yourself. The more you are able to grow your Endogenic strength, the more acutely aware you can be of your surroundings and the more easily you will recognize what state others are in.

When you interact with someone who is constantly in the Exogenic state, the connection between the two of you is missing or artificial. The person can hide things from you, have an ulterior motive, manipulate you and others, or misunderstand the content of the communication without your knowledge. Conversations tend to be one-sided and are dependent on clichés, often full of old jokes, rehearsed, based on assumptions, not relevant to you, manipulative, or self-promoting.

From your Endogenic state, it is easy to recognize the Exogenic state in others. People in their Exogenic states will always have higher tension in their voices, body, persona, and how they relate to the present moment. A person's voice is especially telling. People in their Exogenic states may speak in loud agitated voices, not noticing that unintended listeners can hear them. In the Exogenic state, people's voices commonly have little variation in tone, do not have a flowing resonance, and are prone to sound monotonous, sharp, edgy, or structured. They commonly talk over others, ignoring what someone else just said.

Exogenic interactional behavior can be shrill, rigid, artificial, or repetitious, and never feels warm, generous, or welcoming like Endogenic behavior. From your Endogenic state, you can sense or feel Exogenic tension in ways that could be described as rigidity, pressure, superficiality, detachment, demand, or heightened pace. In your Endogenic state, you can sense Exogenic arrogance, coldness, irritation, or distrust, and you can sense Endogenic generosity, warmth, connection, and empathy.

When you interact with a person, and both of you are in the Endogenic state, you can have a high level of confidence that the person is being authentic and that you are communicating with the greatest possible mutual understanding. Your interaction may be intense, but you will both experience spontaneity, honesty, and clarity with each other. Your communication will be real and without hidden agendas. A person in the Endogenic state can fully process what you say and engage with you completely.

The vast majority of people spend most of their time at work in their Exogenic states. This makes it easy for Exogenic leaders to dominate the workplace. When others are in their Exogenic states, it is easy for highly Exogenic leaders to harness or take advantage of their title, position, or authority by dominating conversations and being on the sending side rather than receiving. Others around them quickly defer to their authority and do not question their motives, purpose, or wisdom. Only those capable of Endogenic observation can see the exploitation.

The most intelligent but overly Exogenic individuals will learn to cover up the distrustful sides to Exogenic behavior. They will learn to make their voices sound relaxed, confident, and pleasing. They will learn to imitate connection and warmth. However, this only works when the others are also in their Exogenic states. The keen Endogenic observer, who can sense Exogenic tension, has the advantage of seeing through cover-ups and can see the behavior for what it is.

To know what state someone is in does not require a checklist or analysis. In fact, that would be an Exogenic approach and would often be incorrect because of the careful cover-ups that highly Exogenic individuals have developed. The only way to really know what state another person is in is to observe from your Endogenic state. The Endogenic observer simply and instantly senses Exogenic tension or Endogenic connection in others and benefits from the knowledge.

When your interactions as a leader include frequent Endogenic moments, conclusions you draw from interactions become more accurate, your communication becomes more effective, and you can better trust the outcomes.

CHAPTER SIX

TIME

*Time is something we have in the Endogenic state and something we
either use up or need more of in the Exogenic state*

In the Endogenic state, time is a resource in which we immerse. In the Exogenic state, time can become an enemy against which we fight. Every moment, the mind engages with the element of time in either the Endogenic or the Exogenic state—may it be by choice or by default. Depending on which state we are in, we have a significantly different experience in that moment, and we are experienced differently by others.

There are three elements to time: past, present and future. In the Endogenic state, we are in the present. In the Exogenic state, we focus on the past and future. Time is something we have in the Endogenic state and something we either use up or need more of in the Exogenic state.

In the Endogenic state, we immerse in the moment. We sense and feel the possibilities that each moment brings, without being restricted by what has happened in the past or what is expected for the future.

When we are in the Endogenic state, time flows without structure. The present moment is undefined and unchartered. We eat when we are hungry, work overtime because we want to, and sleep when we are tired—not when it is time. We are not intimidated by minutes, days, or even a deadline. We are not racing against time and do not worry about not having enough time. We are not constricted by the clock, and with enough Endogenic reliance, we free ourselves from being habitually conditioned to the clock.

In the Endogenic state, time is a resource. Time works in our favor because it constantly renews the current reality. This is why leaders with a strong Endogenic state are able to be patient, not make decisions too soon, and let ideas and solutions unfold when the opportunity allows. The insightful leader knows to keep options open as long as possible because tomorrow will always bring new circumstances and fresh ideas. By balancing hard Exogenic deadlines with space for Endogenic insight, opportunities open up that were previously inconceivable.

In the Endogenic state, one moment may seem to last long and another short, irrespective of the actual number of minutes or hours. The deeper we immerse in the present moment, the more time we seem to have. Many people who have a strong Endogenic state experience deep immersion in the present moment during emergencies. Their sense of time slows down and they can see every detail of the threatening moment unfold in front of their eyes. They are able to think about what to do as if the threat before them occurs in slow motion.

Being in the Endogenic state also brings a perceived slowdown of everyday experiences. An individual with enough Endogenic strength to be fully immersed in the present during a difficult interaction will have the calm and clarity needed to navigate thoughtfully and effectively, without feeling rushed.

Experiencing time in the Endogenic state always ends when we switch to the Exogenic state. We switch as soon as we think about beating the clock, keeping on schedule, or tending to other external demands.

Time has a very different meaning when we are in the Exogenic state. In the Exogenic state, time has structure. We know when it is time to eat, sleep, relax, attend a meeting, take a break, or end a task. We partition our feelings, thoughts, and actions into schedules and time increments. In the Exogenic state, we measure how much we will do by how much time is left. We postpone, delay, and ignore spontaneity. We plan and structure how we use our energy and we protect our down time. If we cannot relax or sleep at the right time, we assume we have too much stress or wonder if something is wrong with us.

In the Exogenic state, everything we think, feel, or do is linked to the past or future in a way that overpowers what the present moment holds. We draw from memories, knowledge, and experience to follow directions, form opinions, focus on goals, and anticipate results. With our focus on the past or future, we may not even notice some of our own present actions or sensations.

In the Exogenic state, time has value. The value we place on time is similar to the value we place on money. We consider how much time something will cost or whether something is worth our time. We think in terms of how we can save time or if we should invest time. We may spend time with someone, take our time, or wish we could buy time. As we count the minutes, we are often reminded that time is money.

In the Exogenic state, time is an enemy. We view time as something we must race against. When we are concerned that time is running out, we fight the clock or beat the deadline. We try to adapt to time by speeding up, or slowing down. We know time is precious, so we try not to lose time and not to waste time. With time as our enemy, we know that if only we had more hours in the day, we could get everything done. Sadly, we seem to never have enough time and we eventually lose our battle against time.

The clock is an Exogenic invention for measuring and structuring time in order to create beginnings and endings. Viewing time this way forces us into the Exogenic state. Following schedules, we create a structured pace and step from one increment to the next. We cut time into sequences and parts that become vessels and placeholders for what we do and experience in life. When we reach a goal, the time that passed as we pursued that goal can seem like a blur. We can be surprised that the day went by so fast or that the children from yesterday are today's adults.

Leaders who habitually overpower their Endogenic state with Exogenic dominance develop a severe underutilization of the present moment. Their work becomes less and less original and they immerse less and less into possibilities that have not been imagined before. As time passes, they lose out on the quality of being. Feeling alive takes immersion in the present moment. The more we fight against time and worry about time disappearing, the more we are building a conflict with time. Our fight against time only leads to Endogenic starvation and exhaustion of the self.

A healthy and powerful view of time must include selectively building on both Endogenic and Exogenic reliance. Only in the Endogenic state are we equipped to grasp the moment, immerse in the present, and unleash creativity. Yet we know it takes structure, planning, and discipline, including schedules and deadlines, to enable output. Time becomes our enemy when we habitually overpower our Endogenic state.

CHAPTER SEVEN

RELIANCE

Much of what we call good or bad luck is the result of being in the right or wrong state at the crucial time

Everyone already relies on both the Endogenic state and the Exogenic state to a lesser or greater degree. This predisposition was determined through conditioning and without our awareness of alternatives or choices. Most of us were raised to rely more on the Exogenic state and to overpower the Endogenic state. The paradox is that overpowering one state results in having less power in our lives, not more.

Endogenic reliance is our capacity to depend on our Endogenic state and Exogenic reliance is our capacity to depend on our Exogenic state. How well each state works for you determines how much you can rely on it. When reliance is strong, you have more choices in life. You can choose which state is most appropriate and effective for any given moment.

To become more powerful, capable, and resilient, you must have strong reliance on both the Endogenic state and Exogenic state. If you have a strong reliance on one state but very weak reliance on the other, you lack resilience and are far more fragile than if you could have strong reliance on both states.

The more you use your Endogenic state, the more familiar you become with it and the more successfully you will use it. When your Endogenic state works, you rely on it more and use it more. The cycle repeats, and the same cycle is true for building Exogenic reliance. Building Duogenic leadership means building both forms of reliance and not neglecting or denying one.

Much of what we call good or bad luck is the result of being in the right or wrong state at the crucial time, and most of the confusion we experience in life is merely a result of not understanding the dynamics of Endogenic and Exogenic reliance. If we could have both Endogenic and Exogenic reliance available at all times, we could avoid the mistake of relying on the wrong state.

The states of Endogenic and Exogenic lead you on characteristically different paths. These two paths produce different outcomes, and over time, they result in profoundly different life stories. When we have thoughts like "I should have trusted myself" or "I should have seen that coming," those are thoughts of regret that occur when we react to a situation in the wrong state.

Since childhood, we have learned to overpower the Endogenic state with the Exogenic state. As this continues into adulthood, if left unchecked, a balance is never reached; the imbalance becomes larger. Individuals without strong and balanced Endogenic and Exogenic reliance never feel safe enough. They feel threatened by anything uncertain, and they address those threats through Exogenic control—even though those threats could often be better addressed in the Endogenic state.

For example, you might have a discussion with a colleague about changing a strategic business decision involving the market prospects for a new line of products. Your colleague may insist the previous decision about market potential should be adhered to, but you have a strong sense that things have changed since then. If your colleague has weak Endogenic reliance, your colleague may insist in staying on course. Without Endogenic reliance, this person cannot face rehashing a previous decision. You trust your introspection on the issue and do not feel locked in to the status quo. With Endogenic and Exogenic reliance, your opinion on business strategy is likely more accurate, yet your colleague without Endogenic reliance will not be able to see that. In fact, your colleague might see you as weak because your point of view appears to change easily, which is hard for someone with weak Endogenic reliance to accept.

A product of Endogenic and Exogenic reliance is that, when both states are highly developed and balanced, you have a much greater capacity for unrest in your thoughts. You can allow yourself to have your opinions disrupted by unsettling things. You can think longer and deeper and take in more complexity. Individuals without strong Endogenic reliance cannot take this unrest because they feel threatened by ambiguity. They prefer a finalized answer over leaving things open. When circumstances test their patience, they resort to opinion and action just to set an end to it. This kind of decisiveness is uninformed. They are rejecting the Endogenic state in themselves out of fear. This is why many decision makers with weak Endogenic states often fail to address the complexity of a challenge adequately.

Building strong Endogenic and Exogenic reliance results in having the ability to choose which state you are in at any given moment. You gain a strong sense of freedom. The choice provides you with the best resources and best approaches to every challenge in life.

ENDOGENIC RELIANCE

Endogenic reliance is our capacity to depend on our Endogenic state. The greater your Endogenic reliance, the less fear you have of your Endogenic state and the less urge you have to avoid it. You build Endogenic reliance by rediscovering how to feel safe while in the Endogenic state. That begins by immersing yourself in the present moment, noticing your sensations, feelings, thoughts, and behaviors in the moment, and not turning away out of fear.

Feeling safe while in the Endogenic state comes naturally when we are young. Children connect with others easily. They create their own experience, their own discovery, and their own direction by relying on their Endogenic state. At the same time, responsible adults are ensuring that children learn what the adults think they need to know, building the children's Exogenic reliance. Some children continue to build Endogenic reliance all the way through adulthood, and others do not. For most, the balance shifts toward valuing the Endogenic state less and depending on the Exogenic state more.

Our degree of Endogenic reliance determines our ability to experience our Endogenic state. Only in the Endogenic state can a person see something and be in awe, be curious, or be touched. A person with strong Endogenic reliance comes up with a lot of new and unique ideas, can listen attentively, easily connects on a deep level with others, is flexible and resourceful, and is compassionate and empathetic.

You very likely have strong Endogenic reliance if statements like the following are often true and are an important part of your character:

- I know how I feel
- I easily empathize with others
- I respond to others the way I feel
- I live in the moment

- I have good intuition and instincts
- I am authentic
- I am usually very open
- I am curious
- I can easily discern underlying concepts
- I am not often misled
- I can detect potential in others
- I can sense when others are lying
- In conflicts, I can easily steer toward win-wins
- I am self-aware
- I comprehend when processes need to unfold
- I can view time as a resource
- I have wisdom
- I am often an inspiration to others
- I can improvise
- I am comfortable being who I am

Endogenic reliance allows you to experience life as it unfolds. It lets you feel a sense of harmony within yourself, where your feelings, thoughts, and behavior feel connected in their own right way. As you learn to depend more and more on your innate strength and on your own resourcefulness, you become more at ease with who you are and you build your Endogenic reliance even more.

Strong Endogenic reliance leads you to know when something feels right or wrong without consulting books or rules. It allows you to know what you value in life, to make important decisions, and to follow your hunches. By relying on the Endogenic state, you do not generically dismiss your thoughts or feelings but rather view them as input that needs consideration.

With strong Endogenic reliance, you accept that what originates within has meaning and value. You are in touch with your own feelings, thoughts, and behaviors and you allow the resourcefulness of the Endogenic state to add to your life. The more familiar you become with your Endogenic state, the more you will develop the varied resources of your self. Consciously choosing to face challenges in the Endogenic state becomes rewarding. This success builds your reliance on the Endogenic state as your personal advancement continues.

Endogenic reliance is the basis for sanity. A common thread among individuals suffering from mental illness is that they cannot feel safe in their Endogenic states. They do not depend on their Endogenic states enough to establish a sufficient balance between Endogenic and Exogenic for effectively dealing with life.

EXOGENIC RELIANCE

Exogenic reliance is our capacity to depend on our Exogenic state. Relying on your Exogenic state comes from active or passive trust in someone or something, including friends, family, coworkers, leaders, science, technology, laws, rules, structures, values, and customs. We actively trust our environment when we choose to trust something or someone and we passively trust our environment when we have an unnoticed dependency, such as the way you trust the motor of a car to start when you turn the key.

Trusting our environment begins the moment we are born. We count on people who provide what we need and want in life. A young child is vulnerable and nearly helpless. Children are eager to seek safety by counting on those around them. Until children have acquired the resources to survive on their own, they want to be aligned with their caregivers. They obey, follow rules, and do what they are asked, even when they do not understand why or do not feel like doing it. They need to depend on others, belong with others, and participate in building collective meaning.

As we learn to depend on others around us and on the rules and structures of society, we become comfortable with looking outward and we rely on our Exogenic state. It is only in our Exogenic state that we build compatibility between our self and the world around us. By relying on our Exogenic state, we can belong to society, count on the resourcefulness of society, make sense to others, and conform to the environment.

You very likely have strong Exogenic reliance if statements like the following are often true and are an important part of your character:

- I am a good planner
- I can be very disciplined
- I know how to give very clear and concise directions
- I can make people follow me
- I put order, rules, and structure in place where needed

- I can keep all of my commitments
- I know how to put hierarchy to good use
- I am a high achiever
- I know how to look the part
- I easily set expectations for myself and others
- I can make others respect me
- If I want to dominate, I will
- I act like a natural
- I can master anything that takes practice
- I can sound like an expert when I'm not
- I collect things that I think are special
- I can get accepted by prestigious groups
- I have excellent organizational skills
- I live by a clear set of values
- I have an eye for detail
- I regard duty and obligation highly

It is easy to develop Exogenic reliance. In the same way children must count on their caregivers for survival, adults want to fit in with society for security and success—so we accept the customs that it requires. We look to others for knowledge, rules, and answers, and we incorporate them in our daily life. When we trust our Exogenic state, we believe that by following the behavior, rules, goals, and beliefs that society presents, we will acquire the things we want in life and will succeed in life. This is alluring and motivates us to work hard, meet expectations, and succeed.

Exogenic reliance lets you trust information you read or hear in books, news feeds, and other sources that you choose to generically accept. Exogenic reliance allows you to follow the methods or rules needed for work and everyday life. It lets you believe that the food you buy in the store is safe, the car you drive is reliable, and the medicine you purchase is trustworthy. It saves you the time and effort of having to question everything, of having to reinvent the wheel, or of having to wonder if what you think or do is correct. It lets you be a conforming member of society who knows the rules and respects the system.

Exogenic reliance allows us to be part of a group united by a common belief, purpose, sense, or loyalty. Exogenic interaction with others creates a common platform between the individual and society. It ensures that we thrive as part of a greater entity that exists outside the self. When we rely on our Exogenic state, we tend to see ourselves in contrast to others in a way that lets us better identify the group we are most aligned with. We seek others who we want to identify with. The peak experience of Exogenic reliance is being part of a group or being part of something bigger than our self. It is a form of identification that we experience as elevating.

As we rely on and comply with society and with the physical world, the repetition of our Exogenic dependence makes us take what we rely on and whom we rely on for granted.

EXOGENIC DOMINANCE

In every given moment, whether you are relaxing or facing a challenge, you are either in your Endogenic or in your Exogenic state. If you do not choose the state, you will be in your default state.

During childhood, we rely on our Endogenic and Exogenic states to different degrees, largely out of our control. We learn repeatedly to not trust all aspects of our self and to trust the rules and beliefs of others. By the time we become adults, a unique mix of reliance on our Endogenic state and our Exogenic state is ingrained in us. For example, we may always rely on our Exogenic state when we are experiencing tension or only rely on our Endogenic state when we are safe at home or when no one else is around.

Without awareness of which state we are in, our default state is firmly established. We continue forward in life as though there were no choice about which state we are in or which state is appropriate at any given time. In certain situations, we default to our Exogenic state, and in certain situations, we default to our Endogenic state. As we repeat our daily patterns, we progressively overpower the state we rely on less. Usually this means our Exogenic state overpowers our Endogenic state. Then, our Endogenic reliance diminishes over time.

When we plan, organize, structure, fulfill expectations, or pursue a goal, we have to rely on the Exogenic state if we want results. If we are in need of a novel idea or long for an aha experience, we have no choice but to rely on our Endogenic state to gain what is fresh and new to us. Using the right state at the right time means tapping into all of our power, but sometimes Exogenic dominance gets in the way. The Exogenic state can overpower the Endogenic state and dominate it. In the Exogenic state, what we otherwise could sense, feel or face, does not occur to us.

Exogenic dominance takes away our choice between Endogenic and Exogenic because our Exogenic reliance takes over, without or against our will, pushing our capacity to be in the Endogenic state away like a bully. Exogenic dominance starts at an early age. A simple example is that we teach children to eat at a certain time even when they are not hungry, so they match their habitual and digestive patterns to the socially structured norms. Boys learn that they cannot shed a tear when they are sad and young athletes are expected to be graceful when they lose a game. We acquire and develop the capability to overpower the Endogenic state from childhood as we learn to adapt, obey, fit in, follow directions, and achieve goals. Every time we cannot rely on our Endogenic state because our Exogenic state will not allow it, we surrender to Exogenic dominance.

You will gain personal power when you begin to question your default state and learn to choose which state you want to be in. Over time, as you use your Endogenic state and Exogenic state in intentional ways, you less often default to your dominant state. The alternative to being in the default state is to choose between the two.

CHAPTER EIGHT

FEAR OF THE ENDOGENIC STATE

Needing to stay busy, planning everything out, and keeping occupied at all times are symptoms of fear of the Endogenic state

The main reason why most people do not rely much on their Endogenic state is that they fear their Endogenic state. The Endogenic state brings powerful emotions, a sense of vulnerability, unexplained spontaneity, and the feeling of insecurity. All the moments in life when we strongly sense and feel something, we are in our Endogenic state. The Endogenic state is not planned, prepared for, or premeditated; such qualities are Exogenic. The Endogenic state is completely real and true to the moment. It can be unsettling to be in the Endogenic state when what we sense or feel is not welcome to us. For example, when we feel vulnerable about our mortality, we may prefer not to know about it. It is scary to sense that there is no certainty to our existence. It can also be unsettling to notice our own feelings of intense anger, pain, sadness, or indifference. Even positive feelings like a strong drive, intense enthusiasm, or unexpected spontaneity can be frightening.

Experiencing our Endogenic state often leaves us wondering if we are in control of ourselves. We do not know how far or extreme these sensations are or if they will embarrass us or endanger us. Anything that is unknown or unplanned can feel threatening. Because we do not understand this unsettling feeling or because of our perceived loss of control, we fight against the Endogenic state instead of embracing it. The result is that we stay in a fear relationship with the Endogenic state.

Facing fear is the key to overcoming limitations and barriers. Fear shows us what our limitations and barriers are, but with a weak

Endogenic state, we become blind to fear. When an Endogenic thought or feeling is frightening, we fight against the fear by rejecting those thoughts or feelings. We simply switch to the Exogenic state.

Only in the Exogenic state can you decide to accept or deny your feelings and thoughts. Denying fear means you do not sense and feel the fear anymore. If you were to switch to your Endogenic state, you would find the fear again. Without even being aware of it, most people develop a pattern of simply avoiding the Endogenic state. Unfortunately, the more we ignore and deny our Endogenic state, the more unfamiliar it becomes, making us fear it even more.

Fear of the Endogenic state can be observed in others. When people switch to the Exogenic state out of fear, they become more uptight, tense, stiff, or scripted, or even rigid, shrill, or abrupt. In the Exogenic state, a person loses flow and warmth. However, the more powerful and intelligent an individual is, the easier it is for them to cover up the signs of fear, and the harder it becomes for others to detect it.

A person in the Exogenic state looks outward for comfort through distractions, food, compensation, rules, habits, and rituals. Needing to stay busy, planning everything out, and keeping occupied at all times are symptoms of fear of the Endogenic state.

Over time, fear of the Endogenic state results in building illusions about life, rationalizing mistakes, fearing change, and missing opportunities for growth. Fear of the Endogenic state is the main growth inhibitor for achieving Endogenic power. By ignoring and denying the Endogenic state, you lose the opportunity to investigate the signals your Endogenic state provides and you look the other way instead.

Fear of the Endogenic State

- You are not aware of your two states
- You feel fear when you sense your Endogenic state in unknown ways
- You conquer the fear with Exogenic tools: ignore, deny, and distract
- Unknowingly, you become weaker and fear your Endogenic state more
- Over time you build illusions, rationalize mistakes, fear change, and miss out on opportunities

---

Fear of the Endogenic state extends to dreams as well. Dreams are a tremendous resource for Endogenic knowledge, but if you fear your Endogenic state, dreams make you uncomfortable. Dreams can be raw and powerful. They arise in the Endogenic state. The Endogenic state makes different knowledge available than the Exogenic state. We are taught from childhood that dreams are not real and have no relevance. We regularly dismiss dreams as meaningless, but actually, we are afraid that they do have meaning.

We extend our fear of dreams to daydreams and intuitions. We often welcome daydreams and intuitions, but as we follow their thread, we may label them as silly. Daydreams and intuitions are easier to handle than dreams. We are less afraid of them because they are usually less encoded. Dreams, daydreams, and intuitions are triggered only in the Endogenic state. While we may not always fear having a daydream or intuition, we often fear taking action upon them. Other than by highly creative people such as inventors, artists, visionary leaders, and entrepreneurs, daydreams and intuitions are most often ignored.

People commonly know little about why they do what they do, think what they think, feel what they feel, or know what they feel. We are afraid of what the Endogenic state generates. When it produces something we do not recognize, we do not want to take responsibility for it. We hear examples of this every day. A person at the office blurts out something that seems out of character—perhaps a mean jab or an odd laugh. Later they tell us they were only kidding or they otherwise refute responsibility for what they said or did. When a person denies ownership of an expression, it is a form of delusion. It is an Exogenic act of clinging to a belief that the Endogenic state does not exist. This may start as wishful thinking, but eventually leads to a distorted reality.

Without understanding the error of ignoring and denying our fear of the Endogenic state, we work hard trying to stay in control at all times. We create illusions, suppress thoughts, rationalize errors, develop blind spots, avoid change, hope to avoid a crisis, limit our growth, and after all that, our fear of the Endogenic state still remains. With this approach, the act of control must be applied at all times. We use our Exogenic state to overpower and lose awareness of our fear of the Endogenic state. Although the fear is controlled, we are not free from the fear. We rely on the Exogenic state, and Endogenic reliance is lost.

Fear and Endogenic reliance can coexist and fuel resourcefulness. A person lacking Endogenic reliance does not experience feeling fear and strength at the same time. Instead, either they are incapacitated by the fear or they attempt to control the fear. It is fight or flight. However, when you are confronted with fear and you are able to switch to your Endogenic state, a feeling of strength arises in you. You suddenly have access to a rush of power and resourcefulness for facing, understanding, or overcoming whatever triggered the fear.

Sigmund Freud concluded that the greatest of all humiliation is to know one is not in control of oneself. His message is that we want to have control over our existence. Avoidance of the Endogenic state and overpowering Endogenic with Exogenic does the opposite of what we mean to achieve. Ultimately, denying our Endogenic state results in a chronic lack of control. By denying our fear, we convince ourselves that the fear does not exist. Once we are not aware of the fear, we cannot learn about it or address it in any way. We lose the access. It is only through developing Endogenic power that we can maximize the control we have in our lives.

OVERCOME FEAR OF THE ENDOGENIC STATE

We will always have fear of our Endogenic state. What we need to consider is that there are two ways to deal with that fear: controlling it in the Exogenic state or facing it in the Endogenic state. It is easy to deal with it the wrong way. An individual who lacks Endogenic reliance turns to the Exogenic state when fearful, but with strong Endogenic reliance, we can face fear in the Endogenic state.

Almost everyone can name some sort of fear in daily life, whether it be fear of water, spiders, darkness, heights, dogs, thunder, needles, flying, small spaces, meeting expectations, or speaking in public. If you have overcome a fear, you probably did it the way most do—through determination. For example, it is common to have the fear of putting one's head underwater. For some, that fear can be strong enough to make you not like swimming, cause embarrassment, or make you wonder if there is something wrong with you. You could overcome that fear by carefully planning a safe way to place yourself in a situation where you could swim underwater, knowing that if your plan worked, you may overcome the fear. If your plan worked, you could repeat the experience, and with continued self-discipline, begin to swim on a regular basis. You could say you overcame your fear.

Another way to overcome such a fear is to discover the fear itself. This is the realm of psychotherapy, but it can also occur on its own, unexpectedly, through experiencing your Endogenic state. Perhaps you are sitting on an idyllic beach with someone you trust very deeply. As you watch the waves and become immersed in the moment, you might be surprised by a spontaneous memory that unfolds and becomes vivid in your mind. You soon realize you are a child in this memory. Perhaps you remember being held underwater in grade school or falling into a bathtub when you were three. If you could stay in your Endogenic state, immersed in the emotion of that vivid memory, you would feel the shock and terror. It may dawn on you that you had found the source of your fear of water. It would come to you as an epiphany and you would feel like a huge curtain had been lifted. You would understand that you were carrying your childhood fear, that the fear was very appropriate back then, and that you do not have to keep the fear anymore.

The difference between overcoming a fear the Exogenic way versus the Endogenic way is that in the first example, the fear is still there. Even though you can control it through discipline, it will still surface at unexpected moments. You may not even be aware of when it surfaces because it may be subtle. It reinforces your fear of the Endogenic state and strengthens your desire for Exogenic control. This impacts your life in ways not at all related to water.

Had you been able to face your fear through your Endogenic state, you would have removed a layer of fear forever. Each layer of fear that you strip away further builds your Endogenic power.

To face your fear of the Endogenic state means to welcome your Endogenic thoughts, sensations, and feelings, and experience that nothing dangerous happens to you while you are in your Endogenic state. Even if your thoughts or feelings are uncomfortable or unexpected, when you can feel safe in your Endogenic state you are getting to know yourself better.

Thoughts and feelings that unsettle you ought to be confronted, not denied. The opportunity is to face conflict between the new and the old or between illusion and reality. It lets you revisit and, if you choose, revise. When you understand your Endogenic state, you will not be afraid that you may unexpectedly act on uncomfortable thoughts or feelings.

When we face our fear of the Endogenic state, we can make a decision about if we should continue facing it and do something about it or forget about it. For example, facing the fear of death may make us live more purposefully, but constantly fearing death will distract and exhaust us. We need to ignore the fear when we are safely buckled in a plane if we want to enjoy the ride or make use of the time. We must choose to either face a feeling

(Endogenic) or override it with thoughts (Exogenic), but doing one when the other would be better is always a waste of time and opportunity. A vast amount of randomness results from ignoring one question: should I be in the Endogenic or Exogenic state at this instant?

The disadvantage of controlling your fear with the Exogenic state is that your denied thoughts and feelings build up like a dam holding back water. Sometimes our Exogenic control weakens—for example, in sleep, under the influence of alcohol, or under stress—and those suppressed thoughts and feelings break the dam. However, when you welcome your Endogenic state, your thoughts and feelings do not build up. They flow and transform. When you face what is going on within you and understand yourself, your feelings and thoughts do not manifest in behavior that you will not understand.

You can also face your fear of the Endogenic state with your dreams. Because sleep breaks Exogenic barriers, being curious about your dreams offers a way to gain insight that is far-reaching. The more you allow for comprehension of the unknown, the more you expand your definition of yourself.

The less you fear your Endogenic state, the more likely you make use of dreams, daydreams, and intuition. If you have a dream that is confusing you, after absorbing the content and understanding it you may be very inspired. Instead of being alienated by the dream, you can benefit from the new information.

You derive direction from intuitions the same way you do from dreams. Intuition is a daily multi-occurrence for someone with strong Endogenic reliance. Overcoming fear of the Endogenic state results in being able to access the power of intuition more easily.

When you welcome your Endogenic thoughts and feelings, you begin to understand the links between your fears and your behavior and they no longer seem random. As events of your life unfold, you can steer them at any moment. Comprehending these connections leads to epiphanies and contributes to psychological maturity.

For example, if you sense that you mistrust someone and you cannot explain why, you might feel uncomfortable making such a judgment. Fear of your Endogenic state may lead you to reject thoughts that seem random or out of place. If you could welcome your Endogenic thoughts and feelings, you would be aware of what leads to the mistrust or you might see it occurring again. You might have noticed a brief moment during a conversation when the other person had a peculiar reaction like looking away, avoiding eye contact, using an irritating tone of voice, having a slightly atypical behavior, or some other disconnection. With your Endogenic awareness, it might have suddenly dawned on you that the other person was lying. That brief moment might have caused the mistrust you felt.

On the other hand, by analyzing in the Exogenic state, you can only reiterate the things that you believe or can prove about another person. If you cannot find any connection between your beliefs and your mistrust, you would disregard your mistrust. By overcoming your fear of the Endogenic state, and welcoming your Endogenic thoughts and feelings, you have much more knowledge to draw from and you can use that knowledge to improve your strategy in future interactions with others.

It is positive to feel insecure and to doubt ourselves. A person with Endogenic reliance lives with question marks all the time about troubling thoughts. Is this the right way? What am I missing? Why am I uncomfortable? What do I want? What is needed? How can I make this better? What is true? These are intelligent questions. They draw intelligent answers. It is invigorating to understand yourself better. You execute with more accuracy than before. Your behavior makes more sense and becomes less random. It increases your confidence, and you can enjoy owning your actions. You know better what you are doing, and you discover a new desire to take risks and do more. Every time you face your fears or insecurities, you welcome, explore, and experience yourself in your Endogenic state. You gain a greater sense of feeling safe and alive as you build Endogenic reliance.

CHAPTER NINE

LEARNING

*Endogenic learning equips you with a keen, uncanny radar to sense
and intuit what is not yet said but in the room, existing but not yet
developed, or unfolding but not yet manifested*

TWO WAYS OF LEARNING

We have two states of being, Endogenic and Exogenic. Learning occurs in both states. Without balancing Endogenic and Exogenic learning, your knowledge—and the breadth of capabilities that result from it—is restricted. Your capacity for wisdom, judgment, and creativity is built from learning in the Endogenic state, while your ability to accumulate facts, follow directions, and replicate the work of others is based on learning in the Exogenic state. Most adults learn predominantly in the Exogenic state.

Exogenic learning is the kind of learning everyone is familiar with. With Exogenic learning, you acquire knowledge by memorizing, accepting definitions, reading, listening, analyzing data, applying formulas, and following directions. You accept new knowledge as fact and trust that it is true and relevant. With this kind of learning, you are seeking to know what is already known. It requires that you be in the Exogenic state.

The other way of learning, Endogenic learning, occurs when you seek meaning. With this way of learning, it is essential that, in the process of acquiring knowledge, you also engage with your senses and feelings. You do this by allowing your curiosity, passion, inspiration, ideas, discovery, and vision to lead the way in absorbing knowledge. It requires that you be in the Endogenic state.

The most striking difference between Endogenic learning and Exogenic learning is that Endogenic learning is based on flow, whereas Exogenic learning is based on structure. A teacher who wants to encourage Endogenic learning knows to appeal to the nonlinear (maybe even disruptive) nature of the Endogenic state by following the moment. This teacher knows to connect to the learners and follow the flow of discovery with minimal structure. On the other hand, a teacher who promotes Exogenic learning begins with structure. This teacher seeks to keep the learners from being distracted and seeks order. From the learner's perspective, Endogenic learning is born out of curiosity while Exogenic learning is driven by necessity.

Whether you rely on Endogenic learning or Exogenic learning is based on the degree to which you have developed Endogenic and Exogenic reliance. Young children do not like to take facts without question. They ask "Why?" repeatedly, searching for understanding and meaning. They insist that answers make sense. Exogenic answers (based on rules, beliefs, or tradition) do not satisfy Endogenic learners. Children's Endogenic states are naturally stronger than their Exogenic states; they start out as Endogenic learners. They follow their own paths of discovery and see the world in wonderment. However, if parents and the environment influence children to become overly dependent on their Exogenic states, they shift from insisting that knowledge makes personal sense to simply accepting knowledge. They gradually rely more and more on Exogenic learning.

A good balance of both Endogenic learning and Exogenic learning is needed for an individual to self-actualize and be a successful leader in a dynamic environment. We are raised to focus on Exogenic learning for advancement, success, and personal growth. Our neglect of Endogenic learning becomes a limitation on flexibility, diversity, agility, intuition, inventiveness, creativity, passion, and growth of the self.

ENDOGENIC LEARNING

Endogenic learning is an experience. By following your curiosity, passion, mood, inspiration, creative ideas, and vision, you process information in a way that lets you make discoveries and reach deep understanding. Endogenic learning builds Endogenic power. You learn things with ease because you follow your interests and your own timing.

As Endogenic learners, we seek to discover. We want to immerse ourselves in the moment and "get it." With Endogenic learning, we do not rely on collective information; we are only concerned with what is meaningful to us. With Endogenic learning, each person learns in a unique way and reaches a unique understanding. When presented with information, Endogenic learners will reject some facts, accept some, and modify others based on how they gauge all aspects of the situation and how it makes sense to them.

When you are in the Endogenic state, you derive information from what you sense and feel and you gain insight into what the present moment holds. You can be aware of what is happening, including what is going on within and outside of yourself, and you have that knowledge at your disposal.

Endogenic learning equips you with a keen, uncanny radar to sense and intuit what is not yet said but in the room, existing but not yet developed, or unfolding but not yet manifested. It allows for uniqueness in thought, performance, and creativity that appears nonlinear, novel, or disruptive.

For example, during a meeting, the Endogenic learner may suddenly make a connection or realize something of great importance while the Exogenic learners in the room are following a linear progression of thought and do not see how this person came up with such an idea. If the input is welcome, it may be appreciated as an out of the box idea. Endogenic learning can surface previously untapped, unused, undiscovered, underlying, invisible, unrealized, and unfulfilled potential.

Knowing how to access the power of Endogenic learning gives us a source of strength that feels bigger than what we are. It feels humbling. We benefit greatly from newness and uniqueness of feelings, thoughts, and actions because they provide a discovery that we could not plan for. It makes us feel resourceful and meaningful and provides us with a sense of abundance. We refresh in the light of our discoveries and epiphanies and may refer to them as "muse," "source of wisdom," "fountain of youth," or "being in the zone." Endogenic learning is best used where uniqueness, newness, freshness, disruptive change, and a spark of genius are desired.

When you are comfortable with Endogenic learning, you do not shy away from the unknown (for example, an obscure challenge or a lack of knowledge). With confidence in Endogenic learning, the unknown makes you curious and alert, but not overwhelmed, because you are open to learn what you need to know as events unfold. Endogenic learners do not have to rely only on adapting or fitting in. They know how to face a situation with curiosity and all of the resources of the Endogenic state, like nimbleness, openness, inventiveness, connection, engaging in a process, being inspired, inspiring others, and welcoming change.

The highly Endogenic learner is skeptical toward structure and instead prefers to protect a free flow. For example, if an outline is required prior to starting a large project, the Endogenic learner sees this as a meaningless and bureaucratic effort because only by looking back at the project can the steps be traced. Rather than fear the unknown, Endogenic learners are fueled by it.

Endogenic learning increases the diversity of ideas and values in an individual and among groups. It helps build your unique personality, interests, and motivations in life. Endogenic learning is creative and rewarding and fosters lifelong growth. Endogenic learning should be enabled and encouraged by parents, teachers, executives, and other leaders, because without it, people become more and more rigid.

EXOGENIC LEARNING

Getting educated, as society defines it, is mostly a process of Exogenic learning. The emphasis is on memorizing, training, repetition, best-known practices, formulas, recipes, following directions, copying, and replicating role models. Exogenic learning leads to compatibility between the self and society's norms and expectations. It is essential in order to function in society and to gain a competitive advantage for your Exogenic needs (making a living, fitting in, being "knowledgeable," having status, following rules). Exogenic learning builds Exogenic power.

With Exogenic learning, you set standards and goals for educating yourself. You work hard to learn enough to make a good living and to have the role and status to which you aspire. You obtain the degrees and certifications that society offers, and you specialize as your job requires.

Exogenic learning provides you with a huge accumulation of Exogenic skills—such as language, reading, writing, math, science, and daily living skills—and Exogenic knowledge—such as of names, places, events, history, laws, rules, and customs. This framework of orientation is required to find your place in the world. It is very effective and efficient to learn these essentials in life without having to experience and discover them all on your own. We benefit extraordinarily from history and others before us by reproducing, modifying, and scaling what has worked in the past. Exogenic learning provides a quick and predictable path to standardized knowledge. It is best used where repetition, replication, and scalability are paramount.

For highly Exogenic learners, circumstances in life are taken as a given. Exogenic learners are used to accepting external parameters and they seek to either live with them or use the system to their advantage. They rely on the resources of the Exogenic state to accomplish the goal of fitting in to what they have concluded life is like.

The Exogenic learner struggles with undefined moments and looks for structure instead. For example, in a social setting, a highly Exogenic learner will be more comfortable asking pat questions than interacting with another person in an open-ended way.

Exogenic learners use plans and strict processes to avoid anxiety and to counter their fear of uncertainty or the unknown. For the Exogenic learner, the unknown is not fun and should be avoided. The Exogenic learner relies on things that are already known by others. Because our society strongly favors the Exogenic state, a fearful person who carefully manages their fear will appear confident and trustworthy to other Exogenic onlookers.

Exogenic learning teaches us to know what others know and to think, feel, and do what others think, feel, and do. Because of our overuse of the Exogenic state, we count on other people to think the same way we do. We even feel betrayed when we have a conversation with someone or experience an event together and later discover that the other person thinks of it very differently.

COMPARISON

We are either in the Endogenic or in the Exogenic state when learning occurs. The experience and outcome of these two forms of learning are contrasted below.

How Learning Manifests	
Endogenic Learning	Exogenic Learning
Comprehend	Memorize
Explore	Acquire
Create	Adapt
Synthesize	Analyze
Invent	Replicate
Perceive	Define
Experience	Study
Discover	Accumulate
Unfold	Assemble
Spontaneous	Conditioned
Connect	Control
Ponder	Judge
Process	Goal
Aware	Pay Attention
Inspire	Instruct

How Learning Manifests	
Endogenic Learning	Exogenic Learning
Curiosity	Belief
Passion	Discipline
Contemplate	Presume
Ambiguous	Absolute
Unknown	Predictable

DOMINANT EXOGENIC LEARNING

In every given moment, whether you are relaxing or facing a challenge, you are either in your Endogenic or in your Exogenic state. If you do not choose which state you want to be in, you will be in your default state. As you repeat your daily patterns, your default state progressively overpowers the state you rely on less. Usually this means your Exogenic state overpowers your Endogenic state. Most adults have become overly Exogenic learners.

When you see a person who has become an overly Exogenic learner, it is alarming. You recognize that their personal evolution has come to a halt. They look outside of themselves to know how to behave and how to feel. Their life is about interpreting their beliefs as though they are a permanent fixture that needs to be made sense of and adhered to.

The dominance of Exogenic learning over Endogenic learning takes place slowly over many years. Because the Exogenic state is strongly reinforced in our society, we gradually give up on expanding our Endogenic learning. We are not aware of this change if we do not know the difference between Endogenic learning and Exogenic learning. We just know that we keep learning more and more, and we assume we are still learning the same way we always did. Overly Exogenic learners do not think there is any other way to learn.

As we lose touch with Endogenic learning, our learning begins to serve a different purpose than it did when we were young. Instead of discovering the world and ourselves, we start to follow the news, learn from information that is channeled to us, and keep up with knowledge needed for our work. This preference for Exogenic learning leaves no room for unfolding personal potential. We end up thinking we are educated, but a major source of learning capacity is ignored.

Schools contribute to the bias toward Exogenic learning. For the most part, students learn what other people already know. This is how most teaching occurs. Knowledge is being handed down. Every so often, a bit of new knowledge is added or some facts are modified in the hand-me-down pipe. Almost everyone is on the hand-me-down end. Education occurs top-down. Young people get used to acquiring knowledge that is fed to them. Although the process may be interactive, it stays Exogenic. The students are expected to fit the answers within an expected realm of options. The thinking works toward grasping a bigger concept that has already been defined. The Endogenic state does not apply itself.

As we lose balance between Endogenic learning and Exogenic learning, a new pattern becomes firmly established. Now, even when Endogenic learning is more appropriate, it does not occur. We cling to Exogenic learning and think we are doing our best because we still find ourselves in a learning mode. But because we are in the wrong mode, we develop a sensation of emptiness, repetition, and being under- or overwhelmed. This seems unexplained because our Exogenic learning may have produced outstanding success in our career and for our self-image.

It is easy to find examples of being in the wrong learning mode. A product development engineer or scientist who wants to make a discovery or solve a pressing problem has two routes to go. This person knows that discovery requires learning, but most scientists or engineers will unknowingly seek Exogenic learning. The Exogenic approach is to define the problem or goal, gather the latest information on the subject, analyze the data, and use that knowledge to hypothesize a solution. Defining the problem or goal is the most important part when Exogenic learning is applied. We know that scientific knowledge is cumulative, so acquiring the latest research is a constant effort.

For innovation, Endogenic learning has to be part of the process. With Endogenic learning, the power is to start with an open mind. You do not direct your thoughts and actions in a predefined manner. You experience what you learn by following your own curiosity. In the Endogenic state, you can notice when information does not feel right. You might sense that something is missing or some point is based on a wrong assumption. Endogenic learning means being stimulated by what you perceive, being open to discovery, pondering the parts that confuse you, and being able to dismiss parts that do not have meaning to you. It places you in the realm of innovation, inspiration, and vision and brings satisfaction and fulfillment from the act of learning. Obviously, highly technical scientific, medical, or engineering discoveries require both Endogenic and Exogenic learning. However, it is only through Endogenic learning that innovation or discovery occurs. Overly Exogenic learners either get stuck in the data analysis phase or merely apply past discoveries to solve current problems.

THE POWER OF UNCERTAINTY

The main reason why most people do not rely much on their Endogenic state is that they fear their Endogenic state. The Endogenic state forces us to face the unknown and places us in touch with the moment. It brings powerful emotions, a sense of vulnerability, unexplained spontaneity, and the feeling of insecurity. The fear makes us disregard Endogenic learning.

One way that we tend to disregard Endogenic learning is by rushing to conclusions and forming opinions. It is only in the Endogenic state that you can feel comfortable with uncertainty. Uncertainty is a powerful tool for learning because it allows you to continue to question and discover. An individual with a poorly developed Endogenic state is afraid of uncertainty. Usually without realizing it, this person will end uncertainty by forming premature conclusions. When learning, all it takes to end uncertainty is to switch to the Exogenic state. For a person with a weak Endogenic state, the temptation to switch to the Exogenic state is overwhelming. Sometimes we may believe we learned something (or became knowledgeable) when all we really did was come to a premature conclusion driven by the desire to end uncertainty.

Instead of enduring uncertainty and continuing to explore, with Exogenic learning we make up our minds. We fit a square peg into a round hole. In the Exogenic state, we are able to take logical plausible facts and accept them. With Exogenic learning, what we accept as fact does not have to make sense to ourselves. When we reach closure, we accept the knowledge as truth. We forget that we cut the process short.

You can see this when you are learning something new, whether it be about work, politics, health issues, home repair, current events, or news. We tend to learn a lot about one thing in specific and then stop looking deeper. Even if we started with Endogenic learning by following curiosity, most of us quickly switch to Exogenic learning and reach for closure. Soon after that, we tend to forget that we stopped looking and think we know it all. Even those of us who realize that learning never ends will usually forget that we only learned part of the whole. Next, we start to act on our opinions as if there were nothing more to know about the subject. We behave as if we are addressing the whole, but in reality, we only know a fragment. The result is that we stop feeling the need to reassess and we move with Exogenic self-confidence that excludes uncertainty.

Without uncertainty and the need to reassess our knowledge, acting on premature conclusions can lead to bad decisions, narrow-mindedness, rejection of diversity, and clinging to the old. The overwhelming prevalence of premature conclusions is why so many mistakes turn into tragedies.

Take a young boy who is taught to look both ways before crossing the street. When this knowledge is learned in a way that has meaning to the child (Endogenic learning), the child will understand that the importance of looking is to engage in the present moment for seeing what the present holds. The purpose is to gain information about the moment: What do I see and hear? How does the road present itself? Do I feel safe to cross? But the child who learns it the Exogenic way simply whips his head left then right and runs across the street. Only blatant dangers are noticed. All the child has learned is that crossing the street means first moving his head both ways. He runs because the street feels dangerous, but he has not learned how to be safe while crossing the street. He abides by the rule he was taught and does not know that his learning was incomplete. The mandate had not been connected to meaningful personal interpretation. The conclusion from the teaching was that once you have looked both ways, you are good to go. Exogenic learning made him, and his educators, falsely assume that he knew all that was needed, but a child with uncertainty, who still ponders the idea of safety, has learned more.

Once we have learned a lot, we begin to judge more. We may take what we know from Exogenic learning and assume there is nothing more, without considering observation. Premature conclusions disregard all that we still do not know about a situation. Exogenic learning represents theory and similar situations like a template from the past, whereas Endogenic learning represents the very specific instant in the very specific context and its own uniqueness. For this reason, Endogenic learning leads to good judgment in unknown territory and Exogenic learning often does not.

Perhaps you have heard rumors at work that the CEO will be stepping down unexpectedly. You speak with a colleague who has strong opinions about the topic, but the opinions of your colleague seem to be based only on recent blogs. You, on the other hand, feel that your knowledge is partial to the whole and that there could be information missing. You remain uncertain on the matter and do not voice a strong opinion yet. Your colleague might leave the conversation feeling like you do not understand the facts or that you cannot take a stand. Of the two, you are the one who remains more insightful and will be less surprised if more facts are revealed.

Individuals with authority or in leadership positions, such as parents, teachers, business leaders, politicians, and religious leaders carry the heavy burden of personal responsibility for generating mass beliefs and action. Leaders must embrace Endogenic learning to ensure that curiosity remains, learning stays fresh, and knowledge builds rather than limits understanding. An individual who feels comfortable with Endogenic learning knows to question conclusions and keep options open for new understanding. An overly Exogenic learner does not.

THE DUOGENIC LEARNER

We commonly think that someone who can recall a lot of things and knows to represent a lot of knowledge must be a very intelligent person. The intelligence of such a person, however, may only rely on one state of being: the Exogenic ability to memorize and retain data.

Exogenic learning makes you smarter and smarter, as long as you want to keep learning. However, there is an entirely other form of learning that you may be neglecting.

Discovering Endogenic learning can lead to the existence of something new. If you want to lead beyond what is already known, you have to tap into Endogenic learning. You can sense and feel, follow your curiosity, explore, discover, and try things anew that do not have a recipe or formula to follow. Great tasks have often been undertaken when the common belief was that they were impossible. All such discoveries were undertaken in the Endogenic state.

When you rely on your Endogenic and Exogenic states for learning, your life becomes more and more fulfilling as you age. Things become easier for you. Your choices are clearer, your decisions smarter, and your interventions more accurate. You become more in charge of yourself, have more success with others, become more influential, and have more wisdom. You become kinder, more generous and compassionate, and not bitter or cynical. You will strive to pass on the good, reduce the impact of destructiveness, and provide what you have in abundance.

CHAPTER TEN

THE FEEDBACK EFFECT

Exogenic feedback can be useful or harmful to others. It causes the feedback effect

WHAT IS FEEDBACK?

Feedback is the information we gain about ourselves from others. Sometimes we ask for feedback, but most of it occurs unsolicited. The content of feedback is limited to what other people perceive and express. Feedback is delivered deliberately or inadvertently through verbal or nonverbal interactions. It can take the form of a specific comment, a look of boredom, or any signal from others that we take as personal.

There are two kinds of feedback: Endogenic feedback and Exogenic feedback. Endogenic feedback refers to feedback that comes from individuals when they are in their Endogenic states and Exogenic feedback refers to feedback that comes from individuals when they are in their Exogenic states.

Endogenic feedback can help another person acquire self-awareness. With Endogenic feedback, we have no false persona and our status, title, resume, and history are all irrelevant to us in that moment. We are able to connect with others, listen receptively, and be responsive, compassionate, and empathetic. Endogenic feedback motivates the recipient (if it does not, it was not Endogenic). That is why Endogenic feedback sounds constructive even when the message entails that something is missing.

For example, if you need your staff member to deliver a status report on time, but that individual has a tendency to be late, you can choose to use Endogenic feedback instead of Exogenic. In the Endogenic state you do not need to make a person feel bad about what they are doing, you can simply communicate your concerns and needs.

You would engage with this person, exchange views on the problem, and come to an understanding about the reports. It could be that the staff member becomes motivated to get them done on time. It could also be that you discover new information that shows you why it seemed impossible to meet the deadline. You can then take steps toward changing the system or correcting the root of the problem.

Where choice is implied, intrinsic motivation takes place. When you give feedback to someone while in your Endogenic state, you are revealing yourself to that person. You do not just repeat what you have already said or refer to rules and standards. You make it personal, you make sense, and you do not have to become controlling. In all likelihood, a real solution will unfold without creating new stress or animosity.

Endogenic feedback is the feedback to give when you do not want a person to respond in a defensive way. Endogenic feedback can help another person be open to new insight because, even when receiving negative feedback, it is descriptive not accusatory.

Endogenic feedback is not merely conveying a need we have, it is an expression of caring. Endogenic feedback causes a small bonding moment when both parties connect over it in the Endogenic state.

Exogenic feedback, on the other hand, can be useful or harmful to others. It causes the feedback effect. In the Exogenic state, we command, judge, direct, set limits, state expectations, control, compare, demand, define, and contrast. We convey to other people that they should be more this way or more that way. We give feedback that is goal-oriented and that is a product of our own habits. We infer a hierarchy between a superior and inferior. In the Exogenic state, we can think we are not influenced by emotion and personal bias, and we act as if we were objective.

Exogenic feedback is a social force that shapes the beliefs we build about ourselves. Exogenic feedback is necessary in order to help children and adults conform to social norms and boundaries. It informs us about who we are and how we perform in the eyes of others, and it tells us what other people think we could or should become. Exogenic feedback easily has us believe that we are what others say we are. With this belief, a definition is given, and personal development tends to revolve around such definitions.

WHAT IS THE FEEDBACK EFFECT?

The feedback effect refers to the long-term negative impact on personal development caused by relying too much on Exogenic feedback. Other people can only see you through their own particular lens. Their feedback may only represent their own needs. They may not know you very well or may only know you in certain settings. They may be an expert in the subject or they may know very little. The result is that, for building an accurate understanding of yourself, Exogenic feedback is commonly incomplete or wrong. Depending on how old you are and how much you are able to validate feedback from others, wrong and incomplete information shapes your beliefs about yourself and influences your decision-making throughout life.

The Feedback Effect:

- People have a limited view of you from their Exogenic states
- They see you through their own particular lens
- They form incomplete or wrong opinions about you
- They communicate their opinions verbally and nonverbally
- You accept their feedback as the truth
- You form fragmented and wrong beliefs about yourself

Every adult has dealt with destructive consequences of the feedback effect. Individuals get trapped in the feedback effect and limit their natural talents because they were conditioned to do so.

When impressions about yourself are mostly based on Exogenic feedback, your self-image is incorrect. Eventually you become accustomed to your incorrect self-image. When you cannot rely on your own self-assessments in the Exogenic state, you become even more dependent on feedback to judge yourself. You continue to wonder what others think about you and how they may react to you. You continue to want to align with what you think others expect from you. Even if your potential is great, the feedback effect holds you back.

Feedback is a reflection of the person who gives it. The person giving Exogenic feedback may not understand the complexity of the situation and so gives superficial direction with their feedback. It may be because of lack of time, lack of comprehension, not knowing about the impact it would have, envy, or other self-interests. Frequently, people do not try to understand a situation before they give feedback; they just release a tension or aim their opinion at others. Likely, the feedback is communicated as a fact, and its impact is lasting. If we fail to process it critically, we end up with wrong beliefs about ourselves.

Feedback is always partial and reflects only a part of the picture. Therefore, even if the feedback is sincere from the giver's perspective, it does not account for any of the aspects of a person that are unknown or irrelevant to the giver. It is inadequate in representing the truth. With time and repetition, we tend to accept incomplete feedback as pars pro toto, assuming a part is the whole. You create beliefs about yourself from small fragments. The lost elements of your self stay untapped and limit the unfolding of your potential.

In the workplace, managers often receive feedback that is wrong or incomplete. For example, managers who are capable of engaging with authentic power for collaborative leadership (as opposed to relying on directive or positional power) may receive feedback that they lack leadership, are too quiet, or do not know enough. These are common comments made by employees who are a bit insecure and who prefer a boss who gives more direction and tells them exactly what is expected. The feedback was limited by the employees' own shortcomings. If you as the leader took the feedback as a truth, you would give up on teaching the team empowerment, which is the more challenging and potentially more successful form of leadership. The result would be a weakening of their authentic power and lost opportunities for growth in others through collaboration.

ORIGINS OF THE FEEDBACK EFFECT

We seek feedback to satisfy our desire to feel safe. We want to belong and know our place in life. We need to know if what we perceive is real and consistent with the reality of others. We also want to know how much we can rely on ourselves and how much we can deviate from others without threatening our notion of safety. The knowledge counteracts anxiety.

When we are young, the feedback we receive is essential. It equips us with social tools and an understanding of what normality looks like. A desire for feedback is part of our natural curiosity to grow and unfold as individuals.

Children have a strong drive to understand the world and themselves in it. Parents play a large role in how children go about reaching that understanding. Most parents unknowingly function with Exogenic dominance. Their known way to satisfy their child's drive for understanding is by giving lots of direction on who they should be, but they do not help their child discover who they are. Discovering who you are is an Endogenic process, and learning who you should be is an Exogenic process. Most adults raise children to build their Exogenic state and neglect their Endogenic state.

As children learn to depend on their Exogenic states for guidance, they look for answers outside of themselves in the form of feedback from others, especially from those who are older or who they consider authorities. Children are constantly subjected to feedback, and they learn to accept the opinions of others as truth. They become so dependent on feedback that most of them do not learn about other ways to gain knowledge about themselves.

Children cannot know when feedback is accurate and when it is not. Consequently, they end up with Exogenic definitions about themselves that are too generic to be true. For example, a child who is very capable and insightful may often jump in right away to provide helpful guidance to others. Such a person will likely receive feedback that criticizes this behavior and labels it as domineering. But Endogenic feedback would reflect a less generic picture and acknowledge the qualities of being very capable and helpful to others. The child could then understand why enthusiasm is sometimes rejected. Too much incomplete Exogenic feedback leads one to suppress a strength instead of develop it.

Parents provide feedback to their children every day. When a child creates a drawing, the child may feel a lot of joy during the process. That feeling of joy may spark the idea to share this new drawing with a parent. Every parent experiences the enthusiastic display of a new creation from their child. The child comes running, saying, "Look at my drawing!" At this moment, anything a parent says or does is feedback.

If the parent is aware of the need to support the Endogenic state, that parent may tune into the child's joy and share the discovery with a comment like "That house looks so cozy" or "Those are very nice colors" or "This makes me feel sad" or "Did you have fun drawing this?" With caregivers like that, the child can more easily develop creative abilities, acquire an artistic outlet, or even use those skills professionally some day.

If the parent has a weak Endogenic state, that parent will tend to critique the drawing, compare it to others, suggest how it can be improved, or show indifference to what the drawing means to the child. The child may hear comments like "It's pretty good" or "You could color this part better" or "Houses aren't really round, are they?" or "I'm busy now." This child suddenly loses the feeling of joy. The parent may not see this as a conflict. They likely think that their Exogenic ways are necessary because the goal is for the child to improve and to learn what life is like. They are building the child's Exogenic state, mistakenly thinking they are doing all they can to help the child.

Children accept feedback from adults as the truth. If the adult is overly Exogenic, the child learns that things need to be done the "expected way." To adapt to expectations is a function of the Exogenic state. The child may do well in the eyes of others, but creativity fades away by stifling the growth of the Endogenic state. If the next drawing does not produce better feedback, the child may simply conclude that the drawings are not good enough and there is no meaning in continuing.

The long-term results of the feedback effect are that the child learns that feelings of joy and discovery do not lead to producing something good or of value to others. Exogenic reliance overpowers Endogenic reliance. The child learns to not trust their own sense of creativity. Eventually, the child stops following inventiveness and passion when engaging in productive activities or when making critical life decisions.

As adults, we seek feedback to have affirmation from others. We pay close attention to what others say about us or what indirect reactions they have toward us. We want to know if we look good, if what we said was too harsh, or if we made the right decision. We rely on the opinions of others to determine our potential in life and how we fit in with the group. Based on feedback from others, we form beliefs about how smart we are, how much integrity we have, how capable we are, what we should do with our lives, and how we compare to other people.

GIFTED AND TALENTED

The feedback effect is especially harmful to gifted or talented individuals. People who are highly intelligent or have remarkable talents are less easily understood by others. They are subject to even more wrong or incomplete feedback. As children, they are asked to temper their hunger for discovery. They may be punished for appearing disruptive. Their curiosity is perceived as provocation. Parents with weak Endogenic reliance do not know how to handle their probing intensity and demanding drive.

Many gifted children are molded into suppressing their Endogenic reliance, never knowing that they can be more. They are children of parents who never guessed their child could rise to greatness any other way than through their controlling guidance. Every parent wants the best for their child, but parents are unknowing players in the feedback effect.

Gifted and talented children are not nearly as rare as we assume. If more caregivers could strengthen their own Endogenic state and rise above the feedback effect, they would enable far more children to discover their talents.

A gifted child is less likely to find adults who understand where they are coming from. The gifted child learns to understand the world from people who have not transcended the feedback effect. They usually have no choice but to seek feedback from people who are already trapped in a dominant Exogenic state.

Gifted individuals do not necessarily show a clear definition of their gift when they are young. They have not yet figured out how to focus and make use of their gift. Adults who operate from the Exogenic state do not understand the complexity of the child. Instead of responding to the complexity, they respond to a part of it: the part they are able to define. Often that part is nothing more than determining if the child followed instructions or did what was expected.

A child who has greater Endogenic reliance than the parents will often reach conclusions or perform actions that the parents cannot accept. For example, when completing a homework assignment, a child may think it is a good idea to make a cartoon that answers the questions instead of writing a paragraph. The parents may find it difficult to understand how the child got to this particular conclusion. They cannot take the leap of thinking that the child could take the input, process it creatively, and deliver an answer, so they do not ask. They stifle the creativity of their child by providing wrong or incomplete feedback like "You can't do it that way" or "That won't work." This makes it very hard for gifted children to use their talents, especially when they have the complexity of an unusual person that does not often "fit in." Most never guess that they might be smarter or could rise above their parents or teachers. Exogenic feedback tells them the opposite.

Talented and gifted adults who have figured out how to use their talents passionately and successfully have become who they are because they invented themselves through Endogenic growth. Either they had environments that supported their Endogenic reliance or they were able to transcend the feedback effect.

In the workplace when a highly creative thinker is surrounded by less creative people, their creativity should be regarded highly, but more often, the creative thinker will be criticized for not following instructions or not staying within the normal or expected parameters of the workplace. The feedback is not accurate because it only includes the aspects that less creative coworkers can understand. It is incomplete. When creative thinkers are not able to convince others about themselves, either they will absorb this feedback by reshaping their beliefs about themselves, or they will leave. The creative thinker who does not transcend the feedback effect will be less creative.

When Exogenic feedback is your only building block for self-definition, you can never perceive yourself as more than the average of the feedback you receive. We acquire a self-image that keeps within the limits of the beliefs and norms of those we interact with.

TRANSCENDING THE FEEDBACK EFFECT

The key to transcending the feedback effect is to develop the ability for Endogenic self-awareness. Endogenic self-awareness means to experience yourself in the Endogenic state. You must be fully aware of yourself and the moment—knowing what you sense, knowing how you feel, being connected to those you are interacting with, and being cognizant of your thoughts and actions. Endogenic self-awareness only takes place when you are in the Endogenic state. At that moment, as you interact with others, you are not studying, analyzing, or comparing; you are simply in tune with what is and what unfolds in the present moment.

When one is able to experience Endogenic self-awareness, feedback is received in an entirely new light. Because you are in the Endogenic state, you can immediately notice if the feedback you are receiving is Endogenic or Exogenic. Most likely, it will be Exogenic feedback, and you will notice that the person giving the feedback is in the Exogenic state.

With Endogenic self-awareness, you often experience a multi-step process as you transcend the feedback effect.

1. Notice the feedback (for example, a peer says you look confused).
2. Use Endogenic self-awareness (you notice that you are quiet because you disagree with the peer's opinion and you are considering how to respond).
3. Detect the mismatch (you are not confused or weak; the feedback is wrong).
4. Acknowledge the mismatch (different realities coexist).
5. Interpret the message (the peer suggests you need help or that you lack mental capability or maybe wants to deflate you in order to win the argument).
6. Accept or reject (with confidence, you can choose to correct your peer's observation or simply ignore it; you have not formed wrong beliefs about yourself).

Endogenic self-awareness allows you to know if feedback is accurate. Your own observations lead you to notice an incompatibility between what you experience about yourself and what you receive through feedback from others.

When you receive feedback—it could be a comment, a look of boredom, a feeling of tension—instantly enter the Endogenic state by calming down, maybe pausing, and noticing the present moment. It may not be necessary that you defend yourself; just think to yourself "I just received feedback. What is my reality?" Notice what you observe in yourself. Is there a gap between what you observe in yourself and what you receive from feedback? If you keep trying to resolve the perception gap repeatedly and it never comes to a resolution that feels right, then you are in conflict with the feedback and the feedback is most likely at fault. You have used Endogenic self-awareness to identify feedback that, if relevant, should now be questioned and analyzed. You may resolve for yourself that the feedback says more about the other person than it does about you.

Another example of using Endogenic self-awareness to evaluate feedback is when your boss criticizes you. Perhaps your boss did not approve of your suggestion in the executive meeting about disclosing more information to the rest of the employees. You catch a look and comment that sends the message, "Toughen up. We are not going to let emotions influence this." If you take the feedback as fact, you will think that your boss perceives you as weak and you should be tougher, like your boss. What if you instantly observe yourself? Does your own experience of yourself tell you that your emotions overtook the clarity of your thoughts or that you made the suggestion because you felt weak? Are your observations in conflict with the feedback you are receiving from your boss? You can confidently know when the feedback is wrong. You can choose if you want to act on this information or just be aware of it for now. Endogenic self-awareness prevents you from shaping a wrong belief about yourself.

Transcending the feedback effect does not mean ignoring feedback from others. It matters greatly what other people think because their perceptions affect how far your influence goes as a leader. If you decide that the feedback is wrong, you then have the opportunity to ask yourself, "How can I influence them to have a more accurate perception of reality?" You may realize that you need to clarify something, confront the feedback giver, or explain your opinion. Suddenly, you are steering instead of deflating. By transcending the feedback effect, you are using feedback to expand your options instead of limit them.

Through Endogenic self-awareness, your desire to understand yourself can be satisfied and you are not desperate for having others fulfill the task for you. Having a tool of your own for assessing feedback helps you counteract wrong beliefs and strengthens the accuracy of your self-image. Over time, Endogenic self-awareness reverses the damage already caused by the feedback effect.

To transcend the feedback effect, you also have to change the way you give feedback. As you distinguish between Endogenic and Exogenic feedback, you can use both as you give feedback to others. Exogenic feedback can help the person know what you expect. It can feel offensive to the recipient if your expectations are unwanted. Endogenic feedback can help another person acquire self-awareness. It can cause a feeling of embarrassment if the recipient is unfamiliar with the Endogenic state.

To give Endogenic feedback, you must be in tune with the situation and the individual receiving the feedback. Endogenic feedback always confirms the Endogenic state of the person receiving feedback. It helps the receiver recognize their own Endogenic state and gain confidence in the Endogenic state at the moment it occurs. It helps the receiver become self-aware at that moment. Endogenic feedback does not set hierarchical inequities or defining categories.

For example, if a colleague makes a presentation at a meeting, afterwards you could take a couple of minutes to tell that person what struck you about the presentation. Perhaps certain parts inspired you, or were lost on you, or maybe you noticed that others in the room were fascinated with one aspect of the talk. If your observations came from your Endogenic state and you communicate them in your Endogenic state, your comments will very likely strike a chord for the colleague. Your comments may help this person become more aware of how they related to the audience, and may boost their confidence about speaking next time because your Endogenic observations will have been consistent with what the presenter sensed during the presentation.

Endogenic feedback from others should be sought out because Endogenic feedback helps build Endogenic self-awareness. It supports us in knowing that what we can sense and feel is real. With Endogenic self-awareness, we can instantly know when the feedback we are receiving is Endogenic or Exogenic. Without discerning, however, we tend to accept or fight against all feedback as fact.

When you transcend the feedback effect, you can make better use of your intelligence. You know how to access the Endogenic state through self-awareness. This intelligence may or may not show up on tests. It always shows up in traits such as personal depth, strength, resilience, wisdom, leadership-foresight, agility, calmness, and accuracy of judgment. It is the kind of intelligence that results in overcoming the challenges of life, understanding how to go beyond simply getting by, and having the strength to follow one's dreams.

CHAPTER ELEVEN

CONFIDENCE

We wrongly believe that behaving confidently is the same as being confident

UNDERSTANDING CONFIDENCE

You know it when you see a very confident person. But do you distinguish which kind of confidence the person has? One kind of confidence can be trusted and the other cannot. One kind is a rehearsed behavior; the other is based on deep-rooted self-reliance. Most people cannot tell the difference, but you can easily know by understanding Endogenic and Exogenic confidence. Discerning confidence in others and building the right kind of confidence in yourself makes you a stronger leader.

Most people who set out to grow their confidence unknowingly work to increase Exogenic confidence. They actually reduce their balance between Endogenic and Exogenic confidence and eventually lose strength as a leader.

Endogenic confidence and Exogenic confidence are opposites. Endogenic confidence is an expression of your Endogenic self-reliance. The stronger your Endogenic state and the more aware you are of your Endogenic strength, the more clearly you express Endogenic confidence. Others will see it as a genuine, honest, and trustworthy personal power. Endogenic confidence lets an individual rise to the occasion with a strength and radiance that is based on deep self-trust and self-knowledge.

On the other hand, Exogenic confidence is an expression of your Exogenic reliance. The stronger your Exogenic state and the more it overpowers your Endogenic state, the more frequently you will express Exogenic confidence. Exogenic confidence can be rehearsed and perfected to appear as though it is an expression of deep inner strength, but Exogenic confidence is really a behavior that draws from a person's position, status, title, and idea they have of themselves. The more the behavior is perfected, the more one will believe in it.

We wrongly believe that behaving confidently is the same as being confident. If we do not distinguish between Endogenic and Exogenic confidence, we trust them both the same. We make mistakes in matters of decisions, judgments, trust, and beliefs, not knowing why.

Endogenic confidence is the standard that everyone uses for what confidence means: an indicator of inner strength, conviction, wisdom, good judgment, trustworthiness, selflessness, and leadership. Yet much of the confidence you see around you is Exogenic, which is merely the display of confident behaviors. Endogenic confidence can be trusted and Exogenic confidence cannot.

Because everyone has both an Endogenic state and an Exogenic state, we all have both Endogenic confidence and Exogenic confidence. The difference between one individual and the other lies in how well developed each state is within them, the degree to which one state overpowers the other, and how aware a person is of their two states. With strength and awareness, a leader can choose to use Endogenic confidence or Exogenic confidence as the situation demands. Having both and having the power to choose gives a leader the greatest set of tools for success.

Having Endogenic and Exogenic confidence gives you great power. Equally powerful is the ability to discern confidence in others. When you know whether a person is displaying Endogenic or Exogenic confidence, you have much more information about this person (and the moment) than others next to you who do not know the difference. Whether it is at the card table or at the boardroom table, you can more easily choose when to trust and when to not. You can detect the difference between wishful thinking and true conviction. You will see through the facades of Exogenic confidence.

The concept of Duogenic leadership explains confidence as a dichotomy. It describes how we build confidence, how we can assess confidence in others, and how we can use that ability and awareness to lead others, collaborate with others, help others grow, and know when to trust or to follow others.

THE ROOT OF CONFIDENCE

The root of confidence is reliance. The degree to which you are able to rely on your Endogenic and your Exogenic state determines how much of each form of confidence you can have. Relying on your Endogenic state requires that you feel safe in your Endogenic state. Relying on your Exogenic state requires that you depend on the world around you and that you trust what you have learned. The stronger and more balanced your Endogenic and Exogenic reliance, the more capable and resourceful you are as an individual.

Confidence is the outward expression of reliance. We cannot easily see another person's reliance, but we can see their confidence. A way to illustrate the difference between reliance and confidence is to compare it to happiness. We cannot see the feeling of happiness in another person, but we can see a smile or a glow. We can say that a smile is the outward expression of happiness. However, there are two kinds of smiles. One is an expression of feeling happy and the other is an expression of thinking we are happy or acting like we are happy. We call them both a smile. Similarly, there are two kinds of confidence. One is an expression of feeling our Endogenic reliance and the other is an expression of thinking or acting on our Exogenic reliance. We call them both confidence. Endogenic confidence is the expression of our Endogenic reliance and Exogenic confidence is the expression of our Exogenic reliance.

The more Endogenic reliance there is, the more Endogenic confidence will show, and the more Exogenic reliance there is, the more Exogenic confidence will show. To the untrained eye, what shows can look the same, but to those who make a distinction between Endogenic and Exogenic, the difference is glaring.

You can get a quick sense of the roots of your own confidence by asking yourself some questions. These questions look below the surface of how you show your confidence to reveal its Endogenic or Exogenic roots.

Examples of Confidence	
Question	Endogenic or Exogenic
Have you felt confident in being who you are?	Endogenic confidence is an expression of Endogenic self-reliance.
Has your confidence increased when you had stronger people on your side?	Exogenic confidence gets stronger with more confirmation from others.
Have you shown confidence by looking the part?	With Exogenic confidence, we choose to act confident.
Has self-awareness given you confidence in yourself?	Endogenic confidence builds as we become aware of our Endogenic strength.
Have you used study and rehearsal to increase your confidence?	Exogenic confidence builds from knowing that we are prepared.
Have you had the confidence to let go of a goal?	With Endogenic confidence, letting go is not the same as failing.
Have you used the memory of your accomplishments to boost your confidence?	Exogenic confidence builds from socially acknowledged success.
Have you been surprised by a situational boost in confidence?	Endogenic confidence shows itself in the moment and is always new and unique.

You can gain more Endogenic or Exogenic confidence focusing on what drives confidence to occur rather than on what confidence looks like. For example, Endogenic confidence can manifest as being humble because Endogenic strength does not rely on impressing others. Exogenic confidence can manifest as being grandiose because Exogenic strength comes through comparison to others and advancing in perceived hierarchies. The opposing forces of Endogenic and Exogenic make up the entire spectrum of self-confidence. Below are examples of how Endogenic and Exogenic confidence can manifest.

How Endogenic Confidence Manifests	How Exogenic Confidence Manifests
Authentic self	Ideal self
Personable	Composed
Essence	Appearance
Self-reliant	Prepared
Spontaneous	Rehearsed
Charismatic	Bigger than life
Modest	Prestigious
Inclusive	Hierarchical
Open	Decisive
Empathic	Charitable
Loved	Admired for accomplishments
Genuine	Manipulative
Unassuming	Polished
Influential	Authoritative
Trusted	Feared

How Endogenic Confidence Manifests	How Exogenic Confidence Manifests
Inspires	Directs
Seeks meaning	Accepts proof
Discovers	Defines
Honest	Loyal
Reliable	Predictable
Feels joy	Has pride

BUILDING ENDOGENIC CONFIDENCE

Because confidence is the expression of reliance, the only way to build Endogenic confidence is to strengthen the Endogenic state.

The stronger your Endogenic state, the more frequently you can experience and express Endogenic confidence. Building Endogenic confidence means building and being an authentic self. It means learning to access your Endogenic state so you may experience the self and its dependability. Endogenic confidence is acquired slowly, through self-growth and awareness. It is fueled by experiencing the strengths you have and by depending on your self.

You can build Endogenic confidence every day by noticing the power of your Endogenic state. For example, when you make a good choice based on insight or when you have a new idea and see it succeed, you encounter the value of your Endogenic state. This strengthens the ease you have with yourself, which increases your reliance on your Endogenic state.

You can strengthen the Endogenic state through curiosity and open and honest discovery of your self. Curiosity in the self results in more frequently noticing your thoughts, actions, feelings, and senses. The act of noticing increases your familiarity with your self. Familiarity with the self gives you greater ease in spotting difficulties, gauging why things are difficult, knowing when you are confused, being less confused, and living each moment with more clarity.

When you reflect on the moment, notice the moment, and feel in the moment, you have placed yourself in the Endogenic state. Being in the Endogenic state gives clarity and allows for better judgment of what is going on inside yourself and around you; misconceptions are fewer, and you are able to appreciate the strength of your self and rely on your self. Relying on your self leads to confidently applying yourself. This all manifests in greater Endogenic confidence.

Building Endogenic strength also comes through better self-care. Nourishing the body and spirit is pivotal. Treating yourself like a best friend, eating well, getting quality sleep, spending time doing things you love, and relating to yourself with respect—this kind of self-care lets you appreciate your self and depend more on your self. In return, you gain Endogenic reliance and you begin to perform better in challenging moments.

One way to experience building Endogenic confidence is to let go of an old goal that is no longer relevant. The Exogenic state is goal-driven. Not reaching a goal is viewed as failure when in the Exogenic state. In the Endogenic state, however, you can gauge if doing less can make space for something even more. In the Endogenic state, you can feel confident about throwing out old goals that are no longer relevant. It does not matter to you if you have invested lots of time or money toward a goal because the Endogenic state is only concerned with what is meaningful to you now. Giving up may be more meaningful than hanging on.

Your Endogenic reliance produces choices that are meaningful to you. This, in turn, opens new doors of opportunity that were not available before. Choices that come from strong Endogenic reliance produce a feeling of relief and renewed energy. You can see and feel how right the choices are and you know you can attribute the success to your choice, not to outside pressure. When you take action on such choices or express your newfound clarity to others, your Endogenic confidence shows. The cycle repeats and builds to form a stronger Endogenic state and greater Endogenic confidence.

People with strong Endogenic confidence have the traits of being humble, open, compassionate, empathic, and personable. Their leadership comes from personal strength, has both substance and appearance, and they tend to share the stage or offer it to others —not because they cannot be in the center, but because they do not feel they have to.

With Endogenic confidence, you are trusted for who you are. Endogenic confidence leads to joy and generosity.

BUILDING EXOGENIC CONFIDENCE

Because confidence is the expression of reliance, the only way to build Exogenic confidence it to strengthen the Exogenic state.

The stronger your Exogenic state, the more easily you can express Exogenic confidence. Your Exogenic confidence is equal to the trust you have in your alignment with your environment. Exogenic confidence draws from knowing how well we perform toward goals and fulfilling the expectations from society and the environment. Exogenic confidence is an accumulation of beliefs gained from the performance results we have achieved in past events.

Your Exogenic state is nurtured from outside. When others are happy with how you perform or how you compare to their beliefs, you gain Exogenic reliance. The more you can fit in, the easier it is to acquire Exogenic reliance. It is built based on comparison with others. Strong reliance on your Exogenic state allows you to behave secure in a situation that you are insecure about. As you gain Exogenic reliance, you build status, image, and pride. We learn how to build Exogenic reliance from childhood, from our social circles, and even more in highly competitive environments.

We express Exogenic reliance in ways that are rehearsed and repeated. Exogenic confidence is a seemingly permanent self-value statement. It declares opinions we have of ourselves. You use your Exogenic confidence to assign positive qualities to your self and hold yourself accountable to these qualities, for example through values and principles. This gives you a sense of strength and pride. You are tempted into acquiring Exogenic confidence because it appears to give you control over your self. For example, you can build an image of who you would like to be and what that needs to look like and acquire behaviors that represent that image. You can build an identity and derive satisfaction from accomplishing what you have built.

We use Exogenic confidence to compete with others around us so we can be braver, smarter, better polished, and more powerful. Because Exogenic confidence is based on comparison to others, as soon as you meet someone who has stronger Exogenic confidence, your confidence crumbles. For example, an expert in microprocessors may be deflated in a meeting with someone who has more knowledge of the subject, or a hierarchy-driven individual who gains Exogenic confidence from towering over others may unexpectedly behave meek when interacting with someone in a higher hierarchical position.

One way to build Exogenic confidence is by acquiring specialized skills or knowledge. Mastering a musical instrument, becoming a winning athlete, being an expert in some field, or knowing more than others about current events all leads to greater Exogenic confidence. With Exogenic confidence, you will be trusted for how you appear.

We often build Exogenic confidence by threatening ourselves, challenging ourselves, or making plans or promises. For example, you may decide you must be more forceful or you will not be respected, or you may rehearse how you speak with your boss so you will appear confident.

Too much Exogenic confidence, if not balanced with Endogenic confidence, leads to a false self, arrogance, and self-aggrandizement. Most highly ambitious individuals have developed very strong Exogenic confidence, often in combination with a lack of Endogenic confidence. Our parents, schools, businesses, and society teach us to pursue Exogenic confidence. We equate confidence with success. We learn, even from childhood, that it is smart to "fake it till you make it," which is the ultimate surrender to Exogenic confidence.

Exogenic confidence is, under the microscope, a set of behaviors that can be studied, emulated, trained, rehearsed, and premeditated. Any ambitious person with self-control can, if desired, obtain the traits of Exogenic confidence through practice and disciplined deployment. Exogenic confidence includes behaviors that mimic the appearance of Endogenic confidence such as the following:

- Body language (for example, clasping your hands in front of your stomach, maintaining eye contact, tilting your head back, making your fingertips touch, walking briskly)
- Relaxed impression (for example, not fidgeting, staying calm, easily accepting criticism, not losing your temper)
- Standing out (for example, appearing taller, being in front, being louder than others, being quick to respond, offering to take charge, being energetic)
- Assertiveness (for example, stating your opinion clearly, being able to say no, being decisive, speaking with well-structured phrases, not letting things slide, standing up for your rights)

There are ample resources available that can help you build Exogenic confidence. Almost any book or management course about confidence, if analyzed, is really about building Exogenic confidence.

It is important to remember that when learning to increase Exogenic confidence, you must not lose sight of the fact that Exogenic confidence is not the highest level of confidence. If you do not also build Endogenic confidence, you quickly become overburdened with the responsibility of knowing how to think, feel, and act as you are expected to.

Constantly applying all the principles of Exogenic confidence builds a facade. If not balanced with Endogenic confidence, the imbalance creates a void that attacks the foundation of your personality. Thoughts like "It's all just a game" or "It all feels empty" or "I'm an impostor" or "The show must go on" characterize the burden. Focusing solely on Exogenic confidence (as so many leaders do), actually builds insecurity, because one can sense that everything one has built in life could easily crumble when external factors change. This fear drives people to seek even more Exogenic confidence if that is the only kind they know. Many leaders become trapped in the cycle of pursuing Exogenic confidence. They are only building confidence on training, not on meaning. They miss out on building personal strength from within.

DISCERNING CONFIDENCE IN OTHERS

A person who sees the difference between Endogenic confidence and Exogenic confidence has better judgment and makes better decisions.

You probably already sense both forms of confidence. You may sometimes feel that you can trust someone, while another equally confident person you can not. It may just feel like a hunch, and you may think there is not a reliable way to know. Without certainty, most people ignore such hunches. You can gain certainty by distinguishing between Endogenic and Exogenic confidence.

Most people observe from their Exogenic state, but in the Exogenic state, we only take things at face value. When a coworker says, "I am sure this new approach will work," taken at face value, you may assess that you trust the confidence of this person. Face value implies that you accept the words for the meaning you give them. You do not account for subtle inconsistencies in tone of voice or innuendo. You do not sense whether the person is overly assertive or fearful that they could be wrong. From the Exogenic state, you will be satisfied that you can hold them to their word.

A highly Endogenic leader and a highly Exogenic leader could say the exact same words, and when you observe them from your Exogenic state, they seem identical. Only if you observe from your Endogenic state can you gauge if someone's confidence comes from the Endogenic state or the Exogenic state.

To know if you are observing Endogenic confidence or Exogenic confidence, you must observe others from your Endogenic state. As simple as that sounds, it is a big challenge for people who do not know how to rely on their Endogenic state.

To enter the Endogenic state, you must slow down, relax, and let go of demands. You must turn toward an inner focus to experience your thoughts, feelings, sensations, and behavior at the present moment. As you settle into the moment, time seems to slow down.

The Endogenic state lets us sense and feel; it generates information that is independent from the trained acts or cover-ups that the Exogenic confident person relies on. Observing in your Endogenic state allows you to acknowledge the appearance of confidence in a person while also sensing (not thinking) the meaning it has to you. This is how you get to the substance.

Observing from the Endogenic state keeps you in touch with how the displayed confidence resonates with you. It allows you to discern how you feel around this person: does the confidence feel deep, calm, and reliable or superficial, thin-layered, or perhaps rehearsed? From your Endogenic state, you can immediately observe the difference between Endogenic confidence and Exogenic confidence, because you will sense if the person you observe is in the Endogenic or Exogenic state.

An easy example of discerning the difference between Endogenic and Exogenic confidence is to look for arrogance. Most people can spot the telltale signs of arrogance: the condescending or pretentious tone of voice, the facial posture of self-importance, disinterest in other people's opinions, and the directive behavior. Arrogance is a product of Exogenic confidence. On the other hand, Endogenic confidence comes from deep within the person and flows with the need of the situation at hand. It will never have the signs of arrogance.

DUOGENIC CONFIDENCE

We all have some of both Endogenic and Exogenic confidence, but very few individuals excel in both. Duogenic leadership comes from having both Endogenic confidence and Exogenic confidence, with strength and balance.

Having both forms of confidence in balance always results in a more powerful and authentic leader who knows how to take risks without being random and who can draw from wisdom rather than act from generic rules and trained behaviors. Knowing how to rely on both the Endogenic state and the Exogenic state results in greater emotional, cognitive, and physical fitness and produces greater intelligence, leadership, and innovative success.

Because society trains us to favor our Exogenic state and to override our Endogenic state, most people do not know how to draw on both states purposefully. Most of your limitations in effectiveness and potential come from unknowingly being in the wrong state. As a Duogenic leader, you can consciously choose between the Endogenic state and the Exogenic state depending on what the situation demands. This gives you the option to assess any situation and respond in a way that will either inspire or instruct, influence or direct, seek meaning or follow rules, discover or define—drawing from the Endogenic or Exogenic state at will.

While Exogenic confidence looks confident, it is the weaker form of confidence. Because it is matched to a specific environment, Exogenic confidence erodes when the environment undergoes substantial changes. Exogenic confidence is dependent on stable conditions. This is a problem in fast-paced business environments where change is constant. A leader with mostly Exogenic confidence becomes rudderless when, for example, market conditions change. Exogenic leaders also mistake a threat to their business for a threat to themselves. Their ego goes into a self-preserving mode that generates defensiveness instead of open-mindedness. Without strong Endogenic confidence, such a leader does not have the strength and agility needed to lead through uncertainty and gain a new, better vision. They easily become devastated from losing territory, status, or comfort zones, even when the change was not due to unsatisfactory performance. Sudden changes throw the Exogenic leader into a personal crisis that absorbs large amounts of time and energy. A Duogenic leader is much more agile and adaptable, likely to keep the bigger picture in mind and outperform again in the new world. Endogenic confidence allows you to recover faster from losses because you do not feel like you lost yourself with the change.

It is easy to find a person with extreme Exogenic confidence and very little Endogenic confidence. Look for the individual who is highly specialized, has deep but narrow expert knowledge, is goal-driven, can easily direct others, is a competitive winner, and can quickly acquire status and power. Such an individual, however, will also have many of the following traits: openly and covertly competitive, non-collaborative, overbearing, elitist, rigidly opinionated, overprotective of turf, self-aggrandizing, inflexible, exclusive, dishonest, or threatening, and have numerous blind spots about their effectiveness with other people. The overly Exogenic individual must rely exclusively on rehearsed behaviors, positional power, and practiced lines. For getting ahead, they must always seek to have more knowledge than others or be more trained, more ready, more practiced, or always pleasing the "right" people.

By contrast, extreme Endogenic confidence, if not balanced with Exogenic confidence, can be found in an individual who is highly caring, loving, generous, calm, insightful, and inspiring, but also is reclusive, adamant against being pigeon-holed, out-of-touch with the mainstream, at odds with institutional power, indecisive, unusual, or has difficulty fitting in and fulfilling requirements on time. They must rely on sensing and feeling in the present and working with what the moment allows. The overly Endogenic individual will try to avoid highly Exogenic people and will miss out on opportunities and existing structures and support systems available in society.

Put a group of mostly Exogenic confident individuals together and the effect is that most of them voluntarily place themselves in ranking order to others without having been told who to follow or to lead. Put a group of mostly Endogenic confident people together and the effect is that most will voluntarily place themselves in a coexisting pattern with others, but all wanting to lead. To have a group with members who lead and follow as the situational circumstances demand, the members must be comfortable with both Endogenic and Exogenic reliance.

Most senior managers display their Exogenic confidence. They have learned the wrong information about developing personal strength and power. Many of those who are perceived as established leaders (and whom others look up to) never feel they have filled the imaginary shoes of a confident leader despite having worked hard on gaining confidence. They have unknowingly worked to increase the wrong kind of confidence.

When Exogenic confidence dominates the workplace, unpredicted risks, uncertainty, and disagreements are not being discussed, explored, or embraced. When bad decisions have been made, someone is fired or reprimanded and the system continues its display of Exogenic confidence.

This suboptimal dynamic can be reversed. For that, the leadership of a company must value, promote, and enable Endogenic and Exogenic reliance. By introducing the concepts of Endogenic and Exogenic confidence and strengthening the climate for Endogenic development, management and the workforce will transition into a more powerful organization capable of greater innovation and collaboration, driven by more intrinsic motivation, diversity, and intelligence.

Misunderstanding confidence is not the individual's fault or the fault of their company. It is a systemic problem. School, work, and society have taught us that acting confident is the same as being confident. It has trained us to not see a difference. With both Endogenic and Exogenic confidence, you are a more powerful, resourceful, and authentic leader who outperforms those with mostly Exogenic confidence.

CHAPTER TWELVE

SELF-AWARENESS

Endogenic and Exogenic self-awareness enables you to switch from one state to the other. This is the most important principle of Duogenic leadership

There are two kinds of self-awareness. One kind is about experiencing yourself, and the other kind is about measuring yourself. Endogenic self-awareness and Exogenic self-awareness are opposites. By pursuing both kinds of self-awareness, people bring forth their full potential.

Self-awareness is the door to self-change. You configure and revise your understanding of who you are from the combination of Endogenic and Exogenic self-awareness. Sadly, most people understand their self-worth using only Exogenic self-awareness.

Endogenic self-awareness is experiencing your self. It takes sensing, feeling, and letting thoughts emerge. As it occurs, you know what you sense, feel, think, and do. The outcome is that you perceive yourself in the making of the moment.

Exogenic self-awareness is self-measuring. It is a comparison to a reference point and defines, classifies, and judges. It includes how you expect to be, how you want or do not want to be, and how you think others see you. It often feels like a test because of its comparative nature.

Self-awareness requires observing yourself. At any given moment, you are either in your Endogenic or in your Exogenic state. That means you will always see yourself in two different lights when you draw upon Endogenic and Exogenic self-awareness.

By learning the difference between Endogenic self-awareness and Exogenic self-awareness, you can detect what state you are in. When you know what state you are in, you can choose the state that you want to be in instead of always ending up in your default state. Endogenic and Exogenic self-awareness enables you to switch from one state to the other. This is the most important principle of Duogenic leadership.

The state you are in at any given moment predetermines how you think, feel, and act. Having the power to draw from both and switch from one state to the other gives you exponential leverage as a leader, parent, teacher, artist, innovator, speaker, writer, or scientist and directs how you are able to build relationships, trust, strength, skill, fulfillment, happiness, wisdom, and power to navigate your life.

During childhood, we grow up heavily influenced by Exogenic feedback. We are taught continuously and consistently to rely on Exogenic self-awareness by comparing ourselves to others. To mature as adults and reach our full potential, we need to rediscover the power of Endogenic self-awareness.

ENDOGENIC SELF-AWARENESS

Endogenic self-awareness is the conception of impressions, observations, feelings, or thoughts about ourselves that occur while we are in the Endogenic state. Endogenic self-awareness is triggered by experiencing the moment as we sense, feel, and act. Endogenic self-awareness is not something we force but rather invite. We allow for its occurrence by being in the Endogenic state.

In your Endogenic state, everything you think, feel, or do is connected to the present moment. In that moment, your thoughts, feelings, and actions become spontaneously known to you. You cannot experience Endogenic self-awareness without being in your Endogenic state.

To experience Endogenic self-awareness, you must fully immerse in the moment, not knowing what you will see. If you allow your feelings and senses to lead the discovery, you will trigger Endogenic thoughts about what you sense and feel, whom you are interacting with, and how you are acting in the moment. In that moment, you know what you are doing, how you are doing it, and what it means to you.

In the Endogenic state, you act according to what you sense, feel, and think. Feelings, thoughts, and actions are linked together meaningfully. As you observe yourself in the now, thoughts emerge. The outcome is that you perceive yourself in the making of the moment without comparing, studying, or analyzing.

If you develop a strong capability for Endogenic self-awareness, you will often notice truths about yourself. Without trying to define yourself through comparisons, you come to know yourself through individual moments of introspection and realizations of new thoughts and new ideas about who you are. Those realizations could be about anything, including your strengths, weaknesses, vulnerabilities, beliefs, worth, status, how others perceive you, or how you can change. When your realizations come through Endogenic self-awareness, they will always be entirely true and uniquely yours in that moment. We see ourselves the way we are at the moment.

Endogenic self-awareness is a capability that cannot be copied, memorized, or learned through precise instructions. Endogenic self-awareness always includes the self and the context (environment and others) at any moment in time. Self-awareness fluctuates in intensity; it may heighten or lessen, be prominent or pale. However, when you lose awareness of yourself, you have left the Endogenic state and are in the Exogenic state.

To experience Endogenic self-awareness requires you to be completely open for newness—or open-minded. It is much more difficult to be open-minded when you are tired or overloaded, so it is important to set aside opportunities for this to occur.

Endogenic self-awareness also requires that you are able to feel safe in your Endogenic state. One has to allow for the senses and feelings to lead the act of discerning. The stronger your Endogenic state, the more you will experience and benefit from Endogenic self-awareness.

In the Endogenic state, you are able to see the state of others. You will sense when others are in their Endogenic or Exogenic states, giving you the power to better understand their motivations, authenticity, and insecurities. You also understand your own motivations, authenticity, and insecurities when you observe yourself in the Endogenic state. Only with Endogenic self-awareness can you effectively contemplate or ponder about your life, be introspective, nurture your soul, soothe your emotional pains, or transcend the feedback effect.

EXOGENIC SELF-AWARENESS

Exogenic self-awareness is your recognition in the Exogenic state of how you compare to or are defined by external reference points. In the Exogenic state, everything you think, feel, or do is linked to the past or future. You see yourself on the basis of comparisons and measure yourself by personal or external standards. As soon as you pursue, compare, study, or list, you are in the Exogenic state. You cannot experience Exogenic self-awareness without being in your Exogenic state.

To experience Exogenic self-awareness, you draw from memories, knowledge, and experience to compare yourself to what other people do, say, and expect. You judge yourself by how well you perform in setting goals, executing plans, or accomplishing your ideals. You evaluate what you have done in the past and what you want from the future. Depending on how well you live up to the expectations you measure yourself against, you feel good or bad about yourself.

Through Exogenic self-awareness, you define what you believe to be your strengths, weaknesses, values, worth, status, how others perceive you, or how you can be better. Your definition of yourself will include critiques, obligations, goals, ideals, and comparisons. You may think of yourself as stronger, weaker, smarter, or less sharp than others. You may create standards for what you should be, as in, "I should work harder," "I should eat better," "I should relax more," or "I should socialize more." You may define yourself based on values you believe are important, as in, "I am better than average at driving" or "I don't drink too much."

Exogenic self-awareness can be acquired through listening, memorizing, and copying. Numerous resources are available to support Exogenic self-awareness, such as psychological assessments, career assessments, and self-help books.

In the Exogenic state, you can embody the self you want to be. You can modify the way you feel, think, and behave to be more like the self you want to be. It is a competitive advantage to be able to exemplify the ideals and beliefs that we define for ourselves.

Exogenic self-awareness provides us with a means for fitting into our surroundings and advancing in society. Keeping up with the Joneses is an Exogenic self-awareness function. By paying attention to the circumstances around us, we can assess the gaps and target goals. For example, if we notice that other people at work are dressed a certain way, we may decide to change our look to be more like others or better than others. Or if it is common to hear people talk about how they work for hours on weekends answering email, we may be inclined to work more on the weekend or to talk about it more as well. Exogenic self-awareness can help us break out of social patterns and habits. We can learn new behaviors and identify with a group or social environment of our choice.

Exogenic self-awareness can be a source of contentment. When we behave in a way someone else wants us to, or when we fulfill expectations and see the resulting satisfaction in the eyes of others, we can be pleased with our contribution.

Exogenic self-awareness also contributes to dissatisfaction in life and missed opportunities. As we look for flaws and weaknesses through judging and comparing, and as we attempt to reduce the gap between our ideals and reality, we often fall short of expectations. Exogenic self-awareness traps us into making incremental steps to improve weaknesses instead of recognizing our talents and strengths and discovering new avenues.

For many people, Exogenic self-awareness dominates. It rules the image they have of themselves. With Exogenic self-awareness, you label yourself in generic terms. When those labels are the only measure you have for your self-worth, you tend to repeat the thoughts and behaviors that perpetuate the labels. For example, if you think of yourself as someone who always has the right answer, you may repeat the behavior of needing to have the last word. Or if you define yourself as witty, you may always seek to get a laugh. For the overly Exogenic individual, this repeated behavior will sometimes be inappropriate or annoying to others because it takes Endogenic self-awareness to gauge a situation and sense when timing is right.

Because Exogenic self-awareness always results in judgments about ourselves, in order to feel good about ourselves or to elevate ourselves among others, we learn to accumulate socially valued trophies, including rank, social network, and possessions. The more we lean on Exogenic definitions of self-worth, the more we focus on securing and maintaining our trophies.

DUOGENIC SELF-AWARENESS

For most people, self-knowledge is derived primarily from Exogenic self-awareness. For example, you might define yourself with words like parent, manager, engineer, intelligent, honest, or lazy. Or you might have principles and ideals that embody the person you think you should be, such as friendly, loving, wise, or generous. Exogenic self-awareness is limited to that which you already know about yourself or already have decided about yourself, excluding everything else.

On the other hand, through Endogenic self-awareness, you engage in self-discovery. You can see the self you are, and you can explore your hidden strengths, talents, or possibilities. In the Endogenic state, you are not concerned with labels or self-imposed expectations. Even though you may be a parent, manager, or engineer, in the Endogenic state, you do not have to act like one if you do not see a need.

Duogenic leadership entails having the capability to draw upon both Endogenic and Exogenic self-awareness. We draw strength from both, confirming what we have decided to be true and having the confidence to discover newness at every moment. We perceive ourselves differently in the Endogenic state than we do in the Exogenic state.

As a Duogenic leader, you let both sources of information about yourself coexist. You hold Endogenic self-awareness up against Exogenic self-awareness. For example, you may get feedback that your ideas are usually too far-fetched. That is your Exogenic self-awareness. With Endogenic self-awareness, however, you know that the idea you just proposed is right on target and that you did not communicate it well. You realize that this can happen to you easily and you need to be more diligent in communicating ideas that could be hard to grasp. Having two sources of information about yourself helps you more successfully get your ideas implemented.

Duogenic leaders have the capability to assess every situation and every moment from two vantage points. Drawing from both Endogenic and Exogenic self-awareness results in assessing the self and the surroundings with the greatest possible accuracy.

Any time you form an opinion about yourself or about what is happening around you, that opinion will be partial or flawed if it comes only from one state. Individuals with an overly dominant Exogenic state will have the most fragmented view of themselves. They will develop significant blind spots. For example, overly Exogenic managers might know themselves to be excellent communicators (through Exogenic self-awareness). This may be true when they give instructions, but they may not accept any fault when someone misinterprets their instructions. Without Endogenic self-awareness, it is unlikely they will discover that communication is a two-way street. They will not notice when they lose others in a communication because they rely on being done when they did their part.

To succeed in a competitive world and to have a fulfilling personal life, we must continuously grow intellectually and emotionally. Drawing from both Endogenic and Exogenic self-awareness results in knowing yourself as much as is possible. The better you know and understand yourself, the more you will be trusted for who you know yourself to be. Other people will think of you as reliable, reasonable, flexible, and having high integrity. They will feel safe around you because, over time, they will learn to trust that you are consistently the person they know you to be.

Examples of Self-awareness	
Endogenic	Exogenic
I notice my own breathing or I can feel my heart beat	I should learn to breathe when I am nervous
I like the clothes I am wearing	I am better dressed than others in the room

Examples of Self-awareness	
Endogenic	Exogenic
I can hear background noises like motors or birds	I can easily ignore distractions
I am thirsty or hungry	I eat only at meal times so I won't gain weight
I notice that my leg muscles are tense	I schedule my workouts to keep fit
I sense a pain in my body	I have a strong tolerance for pain
I am aware of my own words as I talk to someone	I should evaluate my performance after a speech
I can hear pain in someone's voice	I am a good listener
I see something familiar and notice it in a new way	I know what to expect
I notice when people are unaware of what they are saying or doing	I need to avoid spacing out
I suddenly comprehend something new	I should work harder so I can solve this problem
I made a decision that seemed impossible before	I can usually make good decisions

BARRIERS TO ENDOGENIC SELF-AWARENESS

‣ The Feedback Effect

People commonly resist Endogenic self-awareness because they do not trust the judgment they derive from their own feelings and senses.

Due to the feedback effect, we have acquired wrong and incomplete information about ourselves by relying on feedback from others who were in their Exogenic states. When impressions about yourself are mostly based on Exogenic feedback, your self-image is incorrect. The result is that you lose Endogenic confidence and learn to not trust your own senses and feelings. This makes building Endogenic self-awareness nearly impossible.

To overcome this barrier, you have to learn to distinguish Endogenic feedback from Exogenic feedback. You can do that by being sure that you are in your Endogenic state. From your Endogenic state, you can sense what state others around you are in. Endogenic feedback is always accurate in the moment. Feedback from others who are in their Exogenic states can be very damaging because it is always incomplete and generic. If you can be in your Endogenic state, your own self-perceptions are more accurate than Exogenic feedback from others around you.

Exogenic self-awareness is prone to blind spots. Therefore, if you rely only on Exogenic self-awareness, you will be totally unaware of certain qualities in yourself, good or bad. If you can find others who have strong Endogenic self-awareness, those individuals can provide Endogenic feedback, enabling you to see your blind spots and help take away the fear you have of your own self-perceptions.

‣ Presumptions

It is a common mistake to gauge once, using Endogenic self-awareness, and then presume that we can continue to depend on that perception being accurate in the future. For example, we rely on someone for a specific need and then presume we can always rely on the person the same way. Or a person let us down in a time of need so we conclude that person will never live up to our expectations. This pattern of presumption is the result of turning an Endogenic perception into an Exogenic belief.

If you have ever had the thought "I should have trusted myself," it reveals that you dismissed your Endogenic self-awareness at a time when it could have been beneficial. As you strengthen your Endogenic state, you become more and more aware of when your awareness comes from your Endogenic state, and at those times, you know you can trust yourself.

In order to exercise good judgment, most people seek to draw conclusions in an objective rather than subjective manner. Wanting to be objective (relying on facts) is a threat to learning Endogenic self-awareness. It is false to presume that a statement shared by many or voiced frequently always carries more objectivity than a statement that is unique.

Subjective conclusions (those based on Endogenic perceptions) often show the greatest level of good judgment, especially when they come from a solid base of Endogenic strength. When you are in your Endogenic state and others around you are not, you are the one who more likely sees the truth.

Presumptions are barriers to Endogenic self-awareness when we do not know that instead of perceiving at that instant, we have an opinion from the past. Without noticing which state awareness comes from, we remain confused about information that awareness delivers. We are conditioned to disregard Endogenic perceptions, so without awareness, we do not make use of them.

▸ A Stranger to Myself

Many professionally and socially successful individuals say they avoid seeing themselves in the mirror beyond what is needed for leaving the house. Some say that when they look in the mirror, they do not know the person they see and immediately stop looking. Some say they do not like whom they see and look away, or they do not like seeing their own imperfections. These are moments of Exogenic self-awareness, because we see our image and judge it. We find no value in seeing the reflection of ourselves.

Seeing yourself in a mirror is an opportunity to discover yourself as you may be seen by others. Not liking yourself, or not embracing yourself as you are, prevents you from being up to date with yourself and developing further. Avoiding seeing yourself in the Endogenic state means you are missing an opportunity for self-awareness.

What if you were to see yourself in a mirror every day with Endogenic self-awareness? You would not be surprised to see that you have wrinkles because you would know how you looked the day before. Your experience of change can be a continuum with you and your environment embedded in it. In the Endogenic state, you can meet the "stranger" in the mirror and become more familiar and trusting of yourself.

▸ Becoming Self-absorbed

A major barrier to developing Endogenic self-awareness comes from the fear of becoming arrogant or self-absorbed. This is because we confuse self-awareness with being self-absorbed. To become aware of one's power is usually disconcerting at first. Honest people wanting to increase their influencing power are afraid of turning into manipulators. They are concerned about how to digest positive information about themselves that they had not been aware of before. If they like what they see about themselves, they wonder if it is going to make them arrogant. Responsible individuals readily question whether it is appropriate to put attention on one's self. This awkwardness comes from a lack of knowledge about self-awareness.

Exogenic self-awareness can lead to arrogance, self-absorption, and self-obsession. Endogenic self-awareness cannot. Exogenic self-awareness is a state of believing, not seeing, of having an opinion, not exploring. However, with Endogenic self-awareness, we do not hold on to anything. We simply accept what we perceive. Endogenic self-awareness is the opposite of self-absorbed.

Arrogance is used to cover-up insecurities that individuals do not allow themselves to become aware of. It stems from an over-reliance on the Exogenic state. With a balance of Endogenic and Exogenic strength, you will find that you can use awkwardness as a signal for when you can open your eyes further—to draw from your Endogenic self-awareness and tap into the present moment.

By understanding the difference between Endogenic and Exogenic self-awareness, the barrier of awkwardness and fear of arrogance is removed. By knowing that arrogance only results from Exogenic self-awareness, you can confidently explore Endogenic self-awareness and begin to grow your strength and perceptive abilities, allowing you to see how you affect others and the effect your environment has on you.

CHAPTER THIRTEEN

POWER TO CHOOSE

Depending on which state you are in, you have a significantly different experience, and you are experienced differently by others

The Endogenic state is limited in itself and the Exogenic state is limited in itself. Each has its own realm of function. Being limited mostly to one, or having no choice over which realm you have access to, is a self-limitation. Learning to intentionally switch from one state to the other unleashes both realms and allows you to radically extend your limitations.

Typically, you are not aware of which state you are in or how you got there. Switching from one state to the other happens frequently without effort and usually without awareness. The power comes when you learn to recognize your state and start to make choices about which state you want to be in.

There is no moment when the mind is not engaged either in the Endogenic state or in the Exogenic state—may it be by choice or by default. Depending on which state you are in, you have a significantly different experience, and you are experienced differently by others.

What if you are about to interact with a coworker who you know is very competitive with you and you have conflicting ideas on a major project. It is common to have relationships at work where you can predict that intense interactions will result in both of you getting angry and defensive. These kinds of interactions are always Exogenic. When you know how to rely on your Endogenic state, you are equipped with two ways to approach this conflict, switching between your Endogenic and Exogenic states. Depending on which state you are in, the interaction takes a different course. If you intentionally choose, you can make continuous decisions about which is smarter.

What would happen if you approached such a situation in your Endogenic state? In your Endogenic state, you will avoid becoming defensive because you will see that this person is attacking you out of fear or out of conviction. You can break through this person's wall of defensiveness because you can connect and seek understanding. In your Endogenic state, you will be able to engage with this person, build a bridge, get on the same page, sympathize with your coworker's opinion without losing sight of your own, and find solutions that build upon both points of view.

On the other hand, if you are convinced you are more right than the other person is and your way must prevail, you could approach this person in your Exogenic state. In the Exogenic state, you can repeat, copy, and enforce what has happened before. You can prepare your argument and approach your conversation in a way that is already established. You do not need to take the risk of trying something you have never tried before. You will probably be in for a heated discussion that may rile you up for the rest of the day, but you may win.

It takes self-awareness to know which state you are in. If you realize that you are in the wrong state, you have the choice to intentionally switch.

To intentionally switch from the Endogenic state to the Exogenic state, you focus on anything other than the present moment—a past memory, thought, feeling, or action, or a future goal, concern, expectation, or comparison. You immediately leave the Endogenic state when you concentrate on the past or future.

To intentionally switch from Exogenic to Endogenic, you first must decide that you want to be in the Endogenic state. You compare how you want to be with how you are. It will take practice to find your own technique, but the result is that you calm down, become aware of your breath, and arrive at the present moment. Meditation techniques can help you discover your own way to switch to your Endogenic state.

It is easier to switch from Endogenic to Exogenic than from Exogenic to Endogenic. For most of us, Exogenic is our default state and most of our waking time is spent in the Exogenic state. The Endogenic state commonly lasts only a few seconds at a time and occurs unnoticed throughout the day. You can increase the duration and you can increase the frequency of being in the Endogenic state at will.

Knowing when to switch can become easy. Consider switching states when you run into a problem or when you otherwise seek to leverage your performance. If what you are doing is not optimal or your current pace does not fit the moment, you know you are in the wrong state. Whatever state is the most effective for the moment is the right state to be in if you desire to live up to your potential. If the moment demands influencing, discovery, or charisma, you switch to your Endogenic state. If you want to control, judge, or define, you switch to your Exogenic state. When you are in the right state, you are comfortable with yourself at that instant and your pace fits the demands of the situation or circumstance.

CHAPTER FOURTEEN

DUOGENIC
LEADERSHIP

*Most people wrongly assume that individuals who are domineering or
directive must be natural leaders*

In our overly Exogenic business world, many Executives severely
lack Endogenic power. This reduces the potential success of a
business. Leaders with strong Endogenic and Exogenic power are
better equipped to lead a company to success than those lacking
Endogenic strength. The best leaders have developed a freedom
of choice between Endogenic and Exogenic and do not
automatically default to their Exogenic state.

Leaders with Endogenic strength are able to approach
challenging situations differently than their overly Exogenic
counterparts. With the option to choose between the Endogenic
and Exogenic states, they do not feel as threatened and do not
jump to fight at every perceived threat. Instead of always reacting
in the Exogenic state, they can gauge the situation at hand and
ponder what approach would best address the circumstances.

For example, when a big decision needs to be made that affects
many people, a Duogenic leader will likely choose to delay the
final decision until the deadline rather than jump to a conclusion
prematurely. With Endogenic reliance, a leader can let time be a
resource, and does not have to cave under pressure or perform a
certain way only because of what others expect.

Having access to both the Endogenic and Exogenic states allows
a leader to have influential strength and provides agility and ease
to be more strategic, proactive, creative, and insightful.
Encouraging Duogenic leadership in an organization opens vast

possibilities for innovation, collaboration, and synergy by tapping into the full potential of leadership.

Exogenic reliance is easy to learn and strengthen in our society. Our educational systems and most management development programs inadvertently teach us to strengthen only one pillar of the self: our Exogenic state. The more executives strengthen their Exogenic state at the expense of their Endogenic state, the more they tend to instruct rather than inspire, control rather than connect, command rather than enable, analyze facts rather than synthesize something new, apply rules rather than invent approaches, form beliefs rather than allow curiosity, rely on past success rather than tune in to awareness of the present, and follow proven recipes rather than seek discovery.

The challenge in advancing Duogenic leadership is that highly Exogenic leaders are fighters and they are difficult to engage with. Their limited range of behavior often dominates. Most people wrongly assume that individuals who are domineering or directive must be natural leaders. Through our lack of understanding, we have created the myth that an imbalanced personality leads to success, and the myth plays out because there are not many leaders who are capable of leading from both a powerful Endogenic and Exogenic state.

In order to foster an acceptance of Duogenic leadership, Duogenic leaders must keep in mind that their way, when it is Endogenic, may not be transparent and may be misread in an overly Exogenic environment. Duogenic leaders need to be explicit when they choose the Endogenic state. This may mean letting stakeholders know that they are addressing a challenge successfully, expressing why they have decided to postpone a final decision, explaining the strategy behind taking a less obvious route, or giving others time to absorb a divergent idea.

Typically, overly Exogenic leaders will see Endogenic choices as weak, but only because they do not understand the power of Endogenic spontaneity, perception, process, influence, passion, contemplation, accuracy, intuition, and insight. Overly Exogenic leaders are quick to recognize the absence of the behavior they expect.

When Exogenic leadership wants to advance qualities such as vision, inventiveness, discovery, agility, collaboration, synergy, and innovation, they do not know how to distinguish Endogenic from Exogenic solutions. For example, a company may recruit senior leaders from the outside with the promise of bringing novelty and groundbreaking methodology with them. However, if those new leaders are dominantly Exogenic, they will repeat the novelty strategies they have used before without bringing the capability of creating an innovative organization.

The more an organization's success depends on inventiveness, the greater the need for people with strong Endogenic states. Conversely, the more an organization's success depends on repetition and scaling of best-known methods, the greater the need for people with strong Exogenic states. All organizations fare best with leaders who can choose between Endogenic and Exogenic according to the challenge.

Individuals with strong Endogenic reliance are more capable of flexibility and change in the face of the unforeseen. They have a much greater capacity for unrest in their thoughts and disruption of their opinions, allowing them to comprehend more complexity and change course quickly.

Duogenic leaders have the ability to address the full complexity of a challenge, resulting in better decisions. Their Endogenic reliance allows them to not feel threatened by change or ambiguity. They do not need to jump to conclusions or resort to opinion or action just to set an end to impatience. When circumstances become vague or ambivalent, they are capable of pondering the landscape rather than suppressing or denying that they do not have an answer.

Duogenic leaders have access to capabilities such as intuitive risk assessment, inspiration, and inventiveness. Their Endogenic reliance lets them be in touch with the needs of the moment. They can face what others may not yet see. They know whether to reflect or to judge, take in what is going on or make a quick decision, or connect on a personal level instead of controlling and commanding.

Duogenic leaders have the option of choice. They are not forced into over-reliance on the Exogenic state. They can choose Exogenic instead of merely defaulting to Exogenic. They can make informed choices between following what has worked in the past and inventing anew. This gives a leader far greater power to influence a successful outcome for every challenge.

The table below illustrates how outcomes can vary depending on whether a challenge or situation is responded to with Endogenic or Exogenic reliance.

Challenge or Situation	Choose Endogenic Reliance	Choose Exogenic Reliance
Create new marketing program	Envision Invent Bottom-up Unexpected	Compare Scale Top-down Predictable
Lead team to take on new challenge	Enlist Evangelize Unleash potential Passion	Own Sell Define goal Command
Expand Business	Opportunistic Curiosity Discovery New Process Exception	Plan Principles Copy Repeat End goal Standard
Interact with others	Personable Connect	Hierarchical Control

Challenge or Situation	Choose Endogenic Reliance	Choose Exogenic Reliance
Collaborate with partners	Win-win	Compromise
Measure success	Self-approval Fulfillment	Reward Praise
Recover from stress	Look inward for replenishing	Look outward for compensation
Confront challenger	Agile	Battle-hardened
Feeling insecure about a situation	Be aware of the doubt	Stick to beliefs
Respond to demands	Mold expectations into greater purpose	Fulfill expectations
Tension at work	Reflect about the tension	Seek distraction
Rebuild confidence	Self-observation	Feedback from others
Find motivation to work	Passion I like to I want to	Duty I should I have to
Meet a deadline	Time is a resource	Time is an enemy
Reduce anxiety	Turn to empowerment	Turn to escapes or addictions
Lead others	Personal authority Influence	Positional authority Direct

Challenge or Situation	Choose Endogenic Reliance	Choose Exogenic Reliance
Receive criticism	Discern criticism Understand	Put on thick skin Submit or reject
Confronted with new competition	Inspires action	Become resentful
Communicate important information	Have meaning Mutual understanding	Rely on the words Face-value
Acquire knowledge	Discern	Compile facts
Strategic planning	White board Brainstorm	Gap analysis Action plan
Seek promotion	Curiosity Resourcefulness	Entitlement Goal

PART TWO:

LEADERSHIP

CHOICES

CHAPTER FIFTEEN

ACCURACY

*With accuracy, a leader can catapult a company or division beyond
what is reasonably expected*

In the business world, accuracy refers to the ability to make the
right decisions at the right time and to later see that those
decisions were right on target. With accuracy, a leader can
catapult a company or division beyond what is reasonably
expected. Accuracy replaces trial and error, randomness, or status
quo. The key to accuracy is to rely on both your Endogenic and
Exogenic states.

In the Exogenic state, we are able to separate ourselves from the
moment. We can focus on the past or future. To ensure accuracy,
we must balance Exogenic knowledge with Endogenic reliance,
so we can quickly integrate perception, instinct, inventiveness,
and influence, with judgment, experience, and control.

Once you have a certain level of intelligence, it matters more how
you use it. If you do not choose which state you are in, you can
only access what your default state can deliver. As a Duogenic
leader, you have higher accuracy in your judgment. You become
stronger over time instead of weaker or burned out. You are able
to repeat your success not by repeating what worked before, but
by seeing the present in context with the past and future.

For example, a manager in charge of new product development
may have developed a good system for evaluating new ideas and
making quick, market-based decisions. Because of past success,
this leader would likely continue with the proven system. With
Exogenic confidence, one repeats the old recipe for success, but
Exogenic confidence steps in the way of accuracy. In the
beginning, this leader did not have an Exogenic recipe, but was

driven by Endogenic passion, curiosity, dreaming, and thinking out of the box, which resulted in getting ahead of the market.

When Exogenic confidence from a previous success starts to override Endogenic reliance, one loses the connection to the present circumstances. This will result in a reality gap between the past and the present, manifesting in unexplained failures. When you lose touch with your Endogenic reliance, you encounter failures even though all the signs along the way are positive according to the recipe for success.

Without Endogenic reliance, you lose accuracy by excluding Endogenic observation. Innovative ideas falling outside of the confines of an Exogenic recipe are quickly rejected. You are more likely to simply repeat or expand on past ideas.

The pressure to perform to expectations drives many leaders to abandon the Endogenic reliance that drove their success. The loss of Endogenic reliance takes place over years and usually goes unnoticed. It is often the reason why people do not like their work anymore. Instead of feeling like being a kid in a candy store, work becomes a constant burden. Accuracy and passion will return as you rediscover your Endogenic state.

CHAPTER SIXTEEN

ACTION BIAS

What many people do when they feel overwhelmed is spring into action

The personal strength of an individual can easily be seen during a time of overwhelming complexity, confusion, or crisis. What many people do when they feel overwhelmed is spring into action. That might sound courageous, but it is usually the wrong thing to do.

Having a bias toward action is caused by being in the Exogenic state. If you are overwhelmed, pressured, or confused and you stay in your Exogenic state, you will quickly build anxiety. In the Exogenic state, we avoid emotions. When anxiety tries to break to the surface, we want to rid ourselves of it. We release anxious tension by reacting to the threat. Action momentarily reduces the anxiety that the threat induced. In the Exogenic state, action bias can be an automatic occurrence that initiates without awareness.

The problem with action bias is that when we spring into action, it is often the wrong action. In the Exogenic state, the action occurs without any introspection, pondering, interaction, awareness of the moment, or vision. It is often merely the shortest route to removing anxiety. Action bias occurs at all levels from a sharp command like "shut up," to major leadership decisions like firing an employee, dropping a supplier, or choosing one strategic direction over another.

It is common for overly Exogenic leaders to be caught in a loop of action bias. They find themselves facing confusion, turning to action, facing more confusion, turning to action, and repeating these zigzags, working hard and running fast. They do not realize that this is a self-created drama. People who lack Endogenic strength will rationalize their action bias, believing that not acting, delaying action, or questioning how to act is passive behavior that lacks courage.

Leaders with an action bias are often respected. They jump into action and propose concrete immediate solutions. When the action makes sense, even just on the surface, other overly Exogenic individuals will support it because it reduces the tension that feels impossible to bear. Paradoxically, we elevate leaders who lack wisdom. Wisdom only comes from developing Endogenic strength.

The alternative to action bias is to tap into Endogenic reliance before any action is taken. In the Endogenic state, you can experience anxiety without being overwhelmed. You can allow confusion to emerge and sense whether action is necessary right away or not. Having the strength to endure anxiety liberates you from acting out of fear and allows you to increase your awareness of the complexity of the problem at hand. With Endogenic strength, you open space and time for crisp perception, allowing you to consider multiple options, differing points of view, and the long-term strategic implications of your decisions.

Without being driven by fear, leaders with Endogenic confidence can let time become a resource. They can more easily understand a complicated situation. Leaders with Endogenic confidence may have to explain to others why an immediate decision is not necessary and may have to ask others for patience while allowing confusion to last a little longer. In the end, what many people call a crisis can become an opportunity, or at least be solved in an intelligent and thoughtful way, when a leader has strong Endogenic reliance.

CHAPTER SEVENTEEN

AMBITION

Endogenic ambition appears the same as Exogenic ambition, but the two do not feel the same

Seasoned hiring managers will readily tell you that they are much more likely to pick a less experienced but "hungry" person over one who has far more experience and credentials but does not seem eager. Instinctively they make the right choice. They are looking for a person with Endogenic ambition. In a corporate setting, ambition is sought after. It fuels competitive behavior and productivity. There is a big difference in results, however, between Endogenic and Exogenic ambition.

Endogenic ambition is a yearning to unfold your potential and apply yourself. It is a feeling that you have more to come, more to grow, more to unfold, or more to be. While you may not know how to describe the more or know where to get it, you know if you are on the right track. Endogenic ambition is expressed as a person's passion, initiative, eagerness, enthusiasm, zeal, desire, wishes, dreams, motivation, or sense of purpose.

You can easily recognize people with Endogenic ambition by how energetic and hungry for life they are. Endogenic ambition is the source of the greatest discoveries, innovations, new forms of art, intellectual advancements, and entrepreneurial pursuits.

People with strong Endogenic ambition appear as if they want to get ahead, but they really want to thrive. They want to know all, feel all, see all, and live fully. If they use the energy they feel inside, they end up accomplishing things. As they pursue new projects, they are not blinded by a narrowly focused drive. They freely adapt, change course, discard previous work, or start in new directions.

Endogenic ambition triggers creativity and inventiveness, but not always. For many people, it leaves them feeling uncomfortable, lost, or even hopeless. These individuals lack Endogenic confidence. They cannot act on their Endogenic ambition so they push it aside or write it off as a pipe dream. Endogenic ambition is dependent on Endogenic reliance. It takes patience and confidence in the self to know that your yearnings help you make the right choices that eventually lead to something good.

The hunger of Endogenic ambition gets satisfied in moments when you sense you are in your element. With a well developed Endogenic state you recognize when the pace and momentum around you has shifted in your favor, or the dynamics of achievement and fulfillment are congruent with how you sense they ought to be. Such situations feel like old friends. They fulfill very deep longings. The fulfillment of Endogenic ambition spreads to others because your passion is contagious, inclusive, and generous.

In contrast, Exogenic ambition is the pursuit of an objective, target, plan, or lofty goal, often with intense focus and sacrifice. With Exogenic ambition, we have a clear mission that has an end point. We can sometimes be obsessed with reaching that goal. The short-term results can be astounding. A person with strong Exogenic ambition can build tremendous single-minded focus on reaching a goal, creating a high likelihood of success.

Strong Exogenic ambition makes us preoccupied with achievements like having a title or rank or achieving a recognizable milestone. Often driven by fear, insecurities, or desperation of needing to get ahead, this direct single-minded focus can make us ineffective when unexpected barriers occur. If the goal is not reached (whether due to luck, competence, or means) those who rely only on Exogenic ambition will see nothing but failure. Disappointment, shame, bitterness, sarcasm, feelings of betrayal, and destructive behavior often follows.

Over-reliance on the Exogenic state is common among ambitious individuals and the long-term dominance of Exogenic ambition can be harmful. Once a difficult or stressful goal is achieved, the goal will often lose its meaning or leave the person empty and asking what the sacrifice was for—without finding an answer. Such crisis leads many highly successful individuals to quit their high positions, or stay with what they have achieved but feel empty inside. They are also more prone to abusing their gained positional power, to compensate for the feeling of having sacrificed so much to attain it.

To the untrained observer, Endogenic ambition appears the same as Exogenic ambition, but the two do not feel the same. Endogenic ambition feels like a yearning or passion, and Exogenic ambition feels like a burden.

When leadership demands agility, sensitivity to change, strategy, and creativity, Exogenic ambition falls far short. It must be balanced with strong Endogenic ambition to give a leader the flexibility to adapt, sense the needs of others, be open to change, and not be blinded by a narrowly focused drive. Equally, leadership driven only by Endogenic ambition will lack the clarity needed for others to follow and understand their roles and responsibilities in the mission. Following Endogenic ambition alone may not produce expected results, or may fall short of deadlines. As a Duogenic leader, you draw power from both Endogenic and Exogenic ambition as the situation demands.

CHAPTER EIGHTEEN

ANGST MACHT DUMM

Fear drives us into the Exogenic state

When we are afraid, we focus on the threat, but this is often the opposite of what is needed. A popular Swiss proverb warns that fear or anxiety makes us stupid ("Angst macht dumm"). For example, fear of your teacher makes you not able to speak up, or fear of your boss makes you underperform because you cannot think on your feet. This is an example of Endogenic versus Exogenic strength. It is a reminder that when we focus on a psychological threat, we often switch to the Exogenic state and lose sight of the bigger picture.

Fear drives us into the Exogenic state. In the Exogenic state we no longer sense, discern, or gauge the complexity in front of us, which makes it impossible to think strategically. It is great for running from a bear, but for strategic thinking, we can react to fear much better by remembering to pause for a breath and to notice what is happening around us. Switching to the Endogenic state will prevent us from freezing or from reacting inappropriately.

One common anxiety in the workplace is to have your work go unnoticed or for someone else to get credit for what you have done. Imagine that you have worked on a new business idea over several weeks and just before you are about to present it, a coworker presents it and takes credit for it as something "the team" has come up with. You may feel very threatened by this and your "Angst macht dumm" approach might be to stay silent or make inappropriate remarks against the coworker. If you could instead switch to your Endogenic state, you might be able to pick up on flaws in the presentation or notice questions that were not properly answered, and strategically interject some comments that would subtly show that you did all the work and you were letting your coworker try to present it.

To focus on a threat requires that we be in the Exogenic state, but to recognize the threat in its parts and as a whole requires the Endogenic state. To best deal with a threat, we need to rely on both Endogenic and Exogenic. We can acknowledge the Exogenic goal—which is to remove the threat—while we sense, discern, and gauge the complexity in the Endogenic state.

CHAPTER NINETEEN

ANXIETY

Anxiety is caused by losing control and choice over how we face
Exogenic dominance

Exogenic dominance causes tension. Every day we are confronted with demands from work, family, social expectations, and expectations you place on yourself. The demands to meet or exceed our own expectations and the expectations of others push us to be in the Exogenic state. Exogenic demands can be limitless, and if we always give in to the demands, we no longer steer our own lives and we begin to lose our sense of integrity. At some point, in order to protect the balance between Endogenic and Exogenic, we reject Exogenic dominance. You may notice this by feeling irritable, agitated, restless, nervous, worried, or tense.

That moment is the key to curbing Exogenic dominance. If you do not want to give in to a pressing expectation or blindly follow what you take as an authoritative directive, you may face a tension between accepting the Exogenic demand and wanting to reject the demand. How you address the tension created by Exogenic demands determines if you will be troubled by Exogenic dominance. For example, you may be expected to perform a certain duty every day at work. Each time, there may be a brief moment when you are irritated or feel tension about having to do this.

When we lack Endogenic strength, we likely give in to an Exogenic demand by ignoring the tension and allowing the Exogenic state to dominate. Slowly, as we give in more and more to Exogenic dominance, we become used to doing so and the tension becomes unnoticed. Once that tension becomes persistent and abstract, anxiety occurs. Anxiety signals that we are the target of a looming threat. Anxiety is caused by losing control and choice over how we face Exogenic dominance. If we are repeatedly forced to stay in the Exogenic state, we build anxiety. The more quickly and easily we give in to Exogenic demands, the less we notice when it happens, and the less we build our Endogenic reliance.

On the other hand, by switching to the Endogenic state when you notice the tension of an Exogenic demand, the tension either dissolves in the moment or transforms into meaningful feelings and thoughts that give you clarity and help you recognize options and choices between the Exogenic demand and Endogenic meaning. You can choose to reject the Exogenic demand or purposely accept it. By steering these moments and freely choosing which state you are in, the tension does not build and anxiety does not develop. It is not easy to switch to the Endogenic state when Exogenic expectations are strong. To do so requires that you build stronger Endogenic reliance.

Anxiety caused by Exogenic dominance keeps getting worse for overly Exogenic adults. When we are in the Exogenic state, we may not know that we have anxiety. When asked if we are nervous or anxious we may respond as if we had just been insulted. In the Exogenic state, anxiety remains abstract because we do not sense and feel what fuels it. The more you stay in your Exogenic state, the less you will feel the uncomfortable feeling of anxiety, so it is tempting to stay in the Exogenic state. A product of unknown anxieties is that we increase the imbalance between Endogenic and Exogenic. We acquire more and more rigidity by adhering to habits, repetitiveness, either-or thinking, and strict structure in our lives.

This works until symptoms occur. Without us realizing the connection to anxiety, symptoms like slip-ups, inappropriate outbursts, overreactions, aggravation, nervousness, restlessness, or sleeping problems begin to surface. The symptoms may appear random or bizarre, so most people again turn away and ignore them by staying more firmly in the Exogenic state. The act of denying anxiety or avoiding to sense it only buries the underlying cause more.

Anxiety cannot be resolved in the Exogenic state. If we start to feel the pain of anxiety, in the Exogenic state we merely distract ourselves through action and hope the pain will not come back. However, the underlying triggers will probably not go away on their own. Instead of trying to get rid of anxiety by avoidance or denial, the focus needs to be on switching to the Endogenic state. Through Endogenic self-awareness, we can comprehend the intensity of the tug-of-war between Endogenic reliance and Exogenic dominance and build Endogenic power.

Children are at a disadvantage when facing Exogenic dominance. They have dependencies on their support systems that force them to defer to Exogenic dominance. They give up their Endogenic reliance for survival purposes. Once adults, they can rebuild Endogenic strength by facing their tension and anxieties and overcoming previously acquired Exogenic dominance.

▸ Overcoming Exogenic Dominance

When we have endured anxiety for years or decades, we need to reverse and overcome the buildup that has occurred by discovering the underlying causes. Feeling or realizing you have anxiety is an opportunity to uncover those causes. We only connect with the causes of anxiety when we are in the Endogenic state. We can detect rigidities that are central to our lives yet seem unnecessary given today's circumstances or are in the way of future personal growth. Uncovering outdated Exogenic mechanisms, while freeing, can at first cause great tension and confusion.

In your Endogenic state, especially when you are in a safe environment, you can welcome the feeling of anxiety. Feeling and being aware of your breath is one way to switch to the Endogenic state. If you breathe in as deep of a flow as your body allows, you may find that you can hold and focus on two contrasting intensities: the tension of anxiety and the flow of your breath. You can sense that the anxiety starts to lose dominance and begins to dissolve as the flow of your breath grows. If you can continue, and give it the time it deserves, you will begin to feel something different from anxiety. You will feel a sense of power within you. When we meet anxiety in the Endogenic state, we feel it not as tension, but as power. The same intensity that threatened you is the intensity you can feel empowered with.

In the Endogenic state, you can be anchored, connected, strong, and self-reliant. You sense and feel. In this state, you are no longer restless and tense. You can think clearly and you can confront what you were threatened by. This is your opportunity to discover the underlying causes of your anxiety. What may follow is an outburst of feelings, memories, and new meanings, and of creative solutions, in either thought or action. You may break through a limit of yours and make a personal change or discovery that reduces or eliminates part of your anxiety. You may realize that you had a flawed theory, made wrong assumptions, or reached wrong conclusions. It may become crystal clear that you are in the wrong job or on the wrong path in life. You may see that a certain worry, rule, relationship, or expectation is driving your life unnecessarily.

It can be a struggle to view anxiety as an opportunity rather than a threat and to discover the power that is dormant in anxiety. It may come with extreme psychological pain and often one feels weaker before one becomes stronger. To empower the self, stay in the Endogenic state and allow the anxiety to arise and unfold, but only as long as you feel safe in your Endogenic state.

For a person with a strong Endogenic state, anxiety rarely builds up for long. Exogenic demands can be rejected and the threat of Exogenic dominance is more easily understood and uncovered. But even the most developed individuals will frequently find the choice between Endogenic and Exogenic to be difficult. How do you choose between job and family, risk and safety, personal satisfaction and the needs of others? It is common for the Endogenic choice to come with guilt or tension because there may be consequences. You may be letting someone down or not meeting someone's expectations. With enough Endogenic strength, you can deal constructively with these consequences and avoid lasting guilt or tension.

Many people assume that those who feel anxiety are weak. The opposite is true. It takes great Endogenic strength to sense when to defend yourself against Exogenic dominance. To attempt it means you rely on your Endogenic state. People with strong Endogenic reliance are more prone to feeling the tension of Exogenic dominance. They do not give in to Exogenic demands blindly. They may feel a strong resistance to anything that requires conformity, obedience, or performance to arbitrary standards. They acutely feel the tension of Exogenic dominance. Only the uninformed can view such sensitivity as a weakness.

Anxiety is always a key to unveiling conflicts, fears, wrong assumptions, hurts, or pains that directly affect your personal growth. When we are interested in personal development, anxiety is the most important and accurate tool for directing our discovery. Tapping into anxiety is extremely rewarding because, in return, we noticeably expand our sense of inner freedom.

CHAPTER TWENTY

AUTHORITY

When Exogenic authority dominates, leaders tend to silence
collaborative problem solving and avoid discussing concerns by giving
directions instead

Most people think of authority as being the power or right to give orders, make decisions, enforce obedience, or have official permission to act in a specified way. We assume we gain authority by earning a rank, title, or reputation, but there is another kind of authority that can be just as powerful yet much more inclusive, authentic, and respectful.

For most people, the bulk of their work life is spent in their Exogenic states. In the Exogenic state, we accept external definitions such as rank, reputation, experience, degrees, and titles as having greater value than our own observations. We defer to these definitions by granting authority to people with a higher status. In the Exogenic state, we participate in creating and perpetuating these distinctions.

In contrast, if you are in your Endogenic state, external definitions are meaningless. You can interact with someone and come to your own decision about the degree and value of that person's authority. In your Endogenic state, you can sense if another person relies on their status, title, or reputation to create Exogenic authority over others. You can sense their inner strength, honesty, and intelligence—and notice if you feel respect for the person or not. When you sense authority in your Endogenic state, you are distinguishing between Endogenic and Exogenic authority.

Knowing the difference between Endogenic and Exogenic authority, and knowing how to see it in others and develop both in yourself, gives you the power to strategically navigate any hierarchical organizational structure. By developing Endogenic authority in tandem with Exogenic authority, you will attract and align with the people who have the highest integrity and most valuable intelligence in your organization. You will see how others posture and use positional power and you will have a more accurate picture of leadership and authority in your organization.

Endogenic authority is the perception by others of the power of your Endogenic state. The only way to have Endogenic authority is to have strong Endogenic reliance and to be in your Endogenic state while interacting with others. With Endogenic authority, you gain respect without asking for it. You simply apply yourself and relate to others without expecting, nudging, persuading, or dominating.

Endogenic authority is not a means to an end. With Endogenic authority, you are not soliciting authority or seeking to elevate yourself above others. People voluntarily defer to you, without consulting social norms and customs, because you connect with them and they sense your strength, knowledge, or wisdom through a striking impression of personal presence.

People defer to Endogenic authority because they sense power coming from an inner strength and calm that they feel is superior to theirs and the norm. They sense and feel that you know what you are talking about, and it influences their action, independent of what rank or achievements you had in the past.

Endogenic authority is essential for leaders who want to inspire and personally motivate others for a mutually appealing and collaborative undertaking. In a business environment, it must be paired with Exogenic authority.

Exogenic authority is the presumed right of one person to have power, control, or influence over others. With Exogenic authority, you expect respect from others because of your position, title, role, or personal history. People surrender to Exogenic authority because of beliefs, social customs, rules, definitions, or laws.

You gain Exogenic authority by earning a rank, title, or reputation, or being known as an expert, having years of experience, or having strong convictions that you impose on others. With Exogenic authority, you can give orders, make decisions, enforce alignment and obedience, or have official permission to act in a specified way.

Exogenic authority creates and maintains hierarchical order and positional decision-making authority. It gives a leader the right to direct others and require them to behave according to a specific definition, expectation, or goal. You can only exhibit Exogenic authority when you are in your Exogenic state. It is especially easy to draw on Exogenic authority when others are dependent on you for something they need or want, whether that be as a parent, teacher, boss, coworker, salesperson, friend, or spouse.

Individuals with low Endogenic reliance who are in leadership positions depend mostly on Exogenic authority for leadership. Low Endogenic reliance even makes highly accomplished individuals feel insecure and unimportant. They can compensate for these insecurities by identifying with a certain status, position, rank, reputation, or experience, to demand deference from others. Exogenic authority is often cultivated because of this driving force of insecurity, which is why extreme Exogenic authority can manifest as abusive behavior.

Leaders who rely on Exogenic authority are most successful when they attract workers who have low Endogenic reliance. Those who lack Endogenic confidence feel insecure and have a greater need to identify with and defer to a greater external power. Following Exogenic authority delegates accountability away from the individual and onto rules or explicit behavioral expectations.

On the other hand, an individual with strong Endogenic reliance can see through Exogenic authority, especially when it feels abusive or inappropriate. When authority feels abusive, it is because you sensed, through your Endogenic state, that there is a mismatch between the Exogenic demands of the authority and the Endogenic weakness of substance, character, or wisdom. With your Endogenic awareness, you can quickly see when leadership is relying too heavily on position and title and not enough on genuine charisma, situational accuracy, or intellectual superiority.

Most leaders desire more authority, but not knowing that Endogenic authority exists, they seek Exogenic authority. As a result, business environments are high in Exogenic and low in Endogenic authority. When Exogenic authority dominates, leaders tend to silence collaborative problem solving and avoid discussing concerns by giving directions instead.

Fast paced, innovative, successful businesses need leaders who have both Endogenic and Exogenic authority. Endogenic authority is not effective enough when there is no Exogenic authority used to structure collaborative results for execution. To use authority effectively, you draw on Exogenic authority when you need control over other people's direction and you draw on Endogenic authority when you do not.

CHAPTER TWENTY-ONE

AUTOPILOT

Autopilot spares us the effort of thinking, engaging, or dealing with the present moment

Many times a day you can find yourself on autopilot. You will not know it is happening until after. For example, you might realize that you just repeated what you said moments before, or you might wonder if you already brushed your teeth. When we are on autopilot, we are locked into replicating established routines.

Autopilot occurs only in the Exogenic state and when behavior or thought is driven by routine and habit. Autopilot spares us the effort of thinking, engaging, or dealing with the present moment. It separates ourselves from experiencing our routine or habit and allows us to perform without much conscious effort and without paying close attention.

When you want to change a habit that occurs on autopilot, there are two ways to go about that change. You can stay in the Exogenic state and train yourself to exchange one habit for another, or you can switch to the Endogenic state and dissolve the routine. The Exogenic approach takes effort and is usually temporary. The Endogenic approach takes Endogenic reliance and makes autopilot impossible.

For example, you might decide that you want to break the habit of frequently criticizing a colleague. In the Exogenic state, you could train yourself to change your behavior. You might decide to keep something positive in mind about the individual to counter your negative thoughts. You would remember to override the negative thought with the positive thought in hopes your criticisms may lessen over time.

On the other hand, the Endogenic approach is to experience what you think and do. By frequently switching to the Endogenic state, you know the instant you start to feel critical or the instant you have a certain thought. That is the moment you will decide what you will do with your feeling or thought. Experiencing only occurs in the Endogenic state. It allows you to have the choice to intervene in your routine. There is no autopilot in the Endogenic state. You choose your course in each moment.

Switching to the Endogenic state is like being an airline pilot who flips a switch from autopilot to manual. Suddenly you feel the controls and sense that you are the one who is steering.

CHAPTER TWENTY-TWO

BE IN YOUR ENDOGENIC STATE

Being in the Endogenic state can seem awkward or like a waste of time, until you start to see the results

You can build Endogenic power by being in your Endogenic state as often as you can. This is the opposite of what we are used to. Most of the time we are in the Exogenic state, and only in special moments do we spend time in the Endogenic state. We almost always have a choice. We can frequently ask ourselves if it would be possible at this moment to be in the Endogenic state. Could I reflect instead of judge, breathe and notice the moment instead of rushing forward, connect with this person instead of control or command? It requires that we have Endogenic confidence and can switch between Endogenic and Exogenic at will.

For example, if you are about to debate an important issue at work, you may start out with great clarity because you feel confident with your own approach on the matter. When you are being challenged in your argument and feel competitively threatened, however, you may easily switch to the Exogenic state to debate your point.

In the Exogenic state, your argument becomes defensive. You rely on what you know from others and repeat points that have been made before. If you could remember to switch to the Endogenic state, you could engage others in an inspiring and passionate argument and find the perfect flow with every word. It is possible to be powerful with either approach, but with weak Endogenic reliance, you will not have the option to choose one path or the other.

When you notice that you are in your Endogenic state, you can build your familiarity with it by allowing yourself to stay in the Endogenic state for just a bit longer than you otherwise would— one small extension at a time. For example, when you talk with an employee and feel a connection in your Endogenic state, but you notice the employee does not understand what you mean, it is likely you will be tempted to start giving instructions and directions. As you are tempted, you could instead refrain and stay in your Endogenic state a bit longer by asking "Does that make sense to you?" or "What are your thoughts on this?" or "How could we go about this?" You will find out where the disconnect is and where you lost your communication connection. Instead of instructing, reengage and listen, even if just for a moment longer than your current comfort zone allows. Being in the Endogenic state can seem awkward or like a waste of time, until you start to see the results.

CHAPTER TWENTY-THREE

BEHAVIORAL CHANGE

As life becomes more and more complex, rather than continuing to be
open to new situations, we become more rigid and set in our ways

Cognitive theories about behavioral modification presume that thought determines behavior, or that change can be achieved by changing how and what we think. We exchange one thought for another or one behavior for another. Habits, expectations, or beliefs can all be exchanged for different habits, expectations, or beliefs. Change resulting from behavioral modification occurs solely in the Exogenic state.

When a person follows instructions, undergoes training, or acquires prescribed skills, the process is Exogenic. Most educational institutions teach future leaders how to build their Exogenic reliance through a process of training and instruction. They learn best-known methods and adopt what is known by others. Exogenic reliance naturally fits into the structured, measurable, repeatable, scalable, accountable, and predictable procedures that corporations are built upon.

Most business leaders keep a single-minded focus on advancing their leadership abilities through Exogenic learning. A simple form of Exogenic learning is to think, "If I copy other leaders, I will become a better leader," or "If I chat more with my coworkers, they will think I care about them." This behavioral approach to leadership development only advances a leader's Exogenic reliance. It does not increase Endogenic power. If you simply chat more, you do not gain appreciation or empathy toward others, but when your capacity for empathy grows as a result of increasing your Endogenic reliance, you will more often engage in conversations with your coworkers out of genuine appreciation. To the unknowing, both behaviors look the same.

In the Exogenic state, a person approaches change by focusing on a goal or a gap that needs to be bridged. Gap analysis is an Exogenic tool that helps define the steps needed to create alignment between what is and what should be. The task is to close this gap, which is approached top-down by defining a goal. Once a behavior matches the desired definition, the gap is closed. The next step may be to make the changed behavior consistent. This is achieved through repeating the desired behavior until consistency is reached. Most children are raised predominantly this way. It is the nature of change in the Exogenic state.

Exogenic change is highly effective in situations where behavior needs to be modified quickly to match specific needs and demands, such as:

- Performance improvement
- Adapting to a standard
- Learning new content expertise
- Correcting career-limiting behavior
- Adjusting to cultural norms
- Reducing legal risks
- Personal development based on stakeholder input
- Increasing favorable perception by coworkers
- Learning best-known methods and standards
- Conforming to a company's culture

Changing behavior is easier than changing what triggers the behavior. For example, a manager who is highly competitive may be motivated by a strong insecurity. The behavior that results could be destructive for the organization because this person may compete with coworkers when collaboration would be more productive. Exogenic change can help this person focus on collaboration and perform the acts of collaboration, but the underlying trigger, in this case insecurity, is unaffected by the behavior. With luck, the insecurity diminishes for other reasons or stays latent. In most cases however, it will gain intensity and manifest in a new, undesirable Exogenic behavior—perhaps this time something more underhanded, like withholding critical information.

Over time, when behavior is only addressed through Exogenic change, the underlying trigger is buried deeper and further away from the possibility of being addressed by the individual. A buried trigger is a blind spot, which causes flawed conclusions, inaccurate decisions, and erratic behavior.

Exogenic change is good for exchanging one behavior for another, but as soon as the individual does not pay attention, or when circumstances become different, the newly acquired behavior may be forgotten or inappropriate. This is one of the traps of Exogenic reliance. As life becomes more and more complex, rather than continuing to be open to new situations, we become more rigid and set in our ways. Life becomes more planned, more premeditated, and less spontaneous. Exogenic change makes it possible for a person to build a disingenuous, fake-it-till-you-make-it existence, and the more we neglect Endogenic reliance, the more we neglect qualities such as authenticity, integration, insight, self-reflection, and awareness.

The limitation of Exogenic change can be seen everywhere in the workplace. For example, a manager might tell an employee to speak up more in meetings. The employee feels threatened, so decides to change this behavior and speak up more in meetings, but not much has really changed.

Approaching this from the Endogenic state has a different outcome. If the manager is not interested in superficial obedience, but wants to get to the heart of the issue, the manager might engage in a discussion instead of making a demand. Together, they may reveal a mutual frustration about the meetings and the fact that they rarely result in clear decisions. The manager may decide to reinvent the format of the meetings to ensure that decisions are made. This kind of change is not Exogenic change. It unfolded from a process that included insight and understanding. In the end, the employee probably speaks up more at meetings, but now it is because the meetings became more meaningful.

CHAPTER TWENTY-FOUR

BOREDOM

Boredom is like an open door that leads to the Endogenic state

Boredom is a feeling that occurs when the Exogenic state reaches an end or is blocked, yet we resist switching to the Endogenic state. This resistance leaves us with an uncomfortable tension, perceived as boredom, from which most people try to escape.

Boredom often occurs when we are in situations that prevent us from being busy with the goals and pursuits of our Exogenic states. Waiting rooms, staff meetings, or time with the family often forces overly Exogenic individuals into conflicts where they must put their tasks on hold. It is common to see such individuals display the resulting tension with nervous tapping, rude comments, or a rapidly bouncing knee.

We commonly avoid boredom by controlling the moment with Exogenic activities. By simply grabbing a magazine, turning on some music, finding something to eat, starting a new activity, or checking your email, you can instantly pull yourself back into the Exogenic state and the boredom goes away. By looking for something to do, say, or think, we distract ourselves with an activity instead of surrendering to what will unfold next.

Fear of the Endogenic state is what makes people view boredom as something negative. Boredom is like an open door that leads to the Endogenic state. Those who fear the Endogenic state see that door as a danger or like a crack one could fall through.

Without fear of the Endogenic state, boredom is an opportunity. It is the beginning of something new that is yet to unfold. It is a moment that reminds us that we have the option to switch to the Endogenic state. In the Endogenic state, boredom eventually gives way to new ideas, new feelings, or new sensations. Boredom is a rich source for creativity if accepted in the Endogenic state.

CHAPTER TWENTY-FIVE

BREATHING

Exogenic dominance forces us to think that what we do not know does not exist

We all have been told to breathe when we are overwhelmed, confused, or in need of strength. Many people have tried it, only to find it to be of little help. People who have tried to breathe deeply but found it of no use did not switch to the Endogenic state. They simply performed the Exogenic act of breathing. There may be a physiological effect, such as sending more oxygen to the brain, but in the Exogenic state, breathing is mostly an exercise that once performed, leaves you right back where you were before.

The benefits of deep breathing depend entirely on being in the Endogenic state. Deciding to breathe deeply can help you switch to your Endogenic state, but ultimately, your Endogenic state must pull you into breathing. Deep breathing is a symptom of being in the Endogenic state. When you switch to the Endogenic state, you immediately breathe deeply. You slow down, calm down, and open up. When you sense, feel, think, and act in your Endogenic state, you experience the benefits people associate with deep breathing and meditation.

If it is too hard to experience your Endogenic state, you might prefer to believe that it is a useless practice or even a joke. Exogenic dominance forces us to think that what we do not know does not exist. Thinking you are in your Endogenic state does not mean you are in your Endogenic state. You must do it, not think you do it.

If Exogenic dominance is in your way, you can use breathing to help you build Endogenic reliance. Notice your breathing more often. You may discover that you are in your Endogenic state more than you realized. As you increase your awareness of being in your Endogenic state, you will start to discover its power and your reliance will grow.

CHAPTER TWENTY-SIX

CHARISMATIC SPEAKING

*Creating this marriage between content and personal truth is a bond
that enables you to say what you mean*

When preparing for an important talk or performance, some speakers rehearse so well that they know exactly how they will deliver a certain message. They know down to the word what they will say, what joke they will tell, and even how the audience will probably respond to a certain question. We might call this person a very good speaker, but not a charismatic one.

To be a charismatic speaker, you need to understand the importance of Exogenic preparation, but most of your mastery depends on your ability to connect yourself with the content you wish to deliver. You use your Endogenic strength to discover what makes the information authentic to your existence. You immerse into the content in a way that touches deep down where the knowledge you want to pass on connects to your own passion or personal truth. Creating this marriage between content and personal truth is a bond that enables you to say what you mean.

When you speak your personal truth and you connect with your audience through being in your Endogenic state, you will have created a bridge for executing the Exogenic content of your message. Your message becomes compelling. You will naturally pause to make the meaning sink in. Your words may send a chill or bring people to tears. Both Endogenic confidence and Exogenic confidence are powerful, and combined they can result in compelling and charismatic events.

Historically, outstanding leaders are on record while in their Endogenic state. For example, Martin Luther King's last speech clearly shows that power. You can sense and feel the effect, especially when he holds the pauses in his speech. His words sink into you and down to a deep true level of your existence. When you feel it that way, it means that you also allowed yourself to be in the Endogenic state (although a racist would stay in the Exogenic state to not feel the meaning).

CHAPTER TWENTY-SEVEN

CLARITY

Being in the Endogenic state at critical times allows you to keep the big picture in mind

Excessive focus on discipline and goals is caused by fear of the Endogenic state. That fear often leads to failure that could have been avoided. Leaders who have never experienced being in their Endogenic state while engaged in a stressful work project will have no idea what advantage it could bring. The mere mention of concepts like clarity, relatedness, reliance, or sensing sound trivial and inconsequential in the context of their Exogenic work environment. These leaders are at risk—both of making big strategic mistakes and of becoming overburdened and burned out.

If you fear your Endogenic state, you will not have the courage to use your Endogenic power when it is most needed. When you manage a difficult project, complexities and challenges arise along the way. When you only have the resources of your Exogenic state, sooner or later you will become sidetracked or make wrong decisions because you will not have the capacity to see paradox, inconsistency, incongruity, conflict, or conundrum without getting confused.

When you do not fear the Endogenic state, you can, even in the most stressful moments, switch out of your Exogenic focus. Being in the Endogenic state at critical times allows you to keep the big picture in mind while you focus on the makings of its parts. You have the capacity to see dichotomies coexist without getting confused. You see shades of gray instead of only black and white. You see facets, aspects, and clusters of parts becoming interconnected. As you follow complexities, connections between single parts and their relatedness to the whole become clear to you.

All along, while you are in touch with a myriad of details within the complexity, you are not derailed by the temptation to latch on to one part and call it the answer. In the Endogenic state, you have the patience and strength to refrain from jumping to premature conclusions. The sooner you switch to your Exogenic state, the less clarity you have in your decision.

With strong Endogenic reliance, you can accept the tension that builds and know that it is good. It is a reminder to stay in your Endogenic state and to breathe deeper and slower. The more powerfully the problem affects you, the more power you draw from within. What guides you is your sense for staying at par with what the challenge demands. The greater the challenge, the stronger sense of Endogenic reliance you can meet it with.

This sort of clarity is not one of control and discipline, but one of awareness and presence in the moment. Leaders with this capability appear remarkably poised in the face of huge risks, sudden change, and unprecedented challenges. Their success is not by chance, even though others who have no clue of Endogenic power may naively think they could have pulled it off just the same.

CHAPTER TWENTY-EIGHT

COLLABORATION

When two individuals communicate from their Endogenic states, a true connection is made

Most people attempt to collaborate while in their Exogenic states. In the Exogenic state, you can dominate and focus on how to convince the other party of what you want. However, since the other party tries to do the same to you, the result is usually a compromise, which means that neither of you walk away with what you wanted. This pattern occurs over and over in business as a standard, yet it is not the most intelligent way to collaborate.

The greatest outcome in relationship building and collaboration always comes through Endogenic reliance. With strong Endogenic reliance, your awareness can pull your negotiation partners out of their Exogenic states and into their Endogenic states. The result is that you both communicate from your Endogenic states. It takes someone with powerful Endogenic reliance to be able to pull others from Exogenic to Endogenic. One-on-one or small groups are best suited for this approach.

When two individuals communicate from their Endogenic states, a true connection is made. You can reach understandings that cannot be reached in the Exogenic state. Endogenic collaboration is synergistic. You can find common ground without losing your advantage and you can find solutions that favor both by giving each other what each side wants instead of taking away. You can explore the areas that do not make sense, find the missing links that keep you from moving forward, and be creative together. Your mutual understanding of a successful outcome pulls from the resources of two, caring for a satisfying outcome, instead of being a fight against each other over a limited resource.

CHAPTER TWENTY-NINE

COMMUNICATION

*Being in the wrong state when we communicate is the main reason
conflicts get messy and escalate far beyond what was originally at stake*

Most people, especially in work situations, communicate while in
the Exogenic state. In the Exogenic state, we think our message is
heard because we said it. Then, we expect the receiver to
understand, or even change, based on what we said. The more
explicit and clear we are, the more we expect to be heard. When
the receiver acknowledges us or indicates that we have been
heard, we assume our message was understood and we base all
further action on that assumption. We act as though our message
was understood, while it might not have been.

Communication can be thought of like a relay baton. The baton
needs to be handed and taken. If you hand it and it drops, that
particular part of communication breaks down. In the Exogenic
state, we only know to hand the baton. We do not know if or
how it was received. In the very moment of passing the baton
from one person to the other, the sender must be in the
Endogenic state to know what happened to the message.

In the Endogenic state, you can sense if a word reaches someone
and how it lands. You can see how the other person absorbs what
you send their way. As you see their reaction, you are connected
to yourself and to them, enabling you to guide your message and
choose your words in a way that respectfully deals with the
barriers the person puts up. You can place your message without
missing openness, if openness can be found.

You can only see if a message is received by someone when you
are in your Endogenic state. You have to sense how you and the
situation affect the person. Thinking about a fictitious baton is
one way to remind yourself to stay in the Endogenic state. You

can immediately sense the difference between Endogenic and Exogenic communication.

If you have something difficult or negative to say, the importance of communicating in the Endogenic state is even greater. During moments of frustration or tension, it is much harder for a person with low Endogenic strength to communicate effectively. In the Exogenic state, we do not gauge what the moment holds. All we want to do is reach the goal. If we cannot switch to the Endogenic state, our communication is hindered by our frustration. Being in the wrong state when we communicate is the main reason conflicts get messy and escalate far beyond what was originally at stake.

Optimal communication needs both Endogenic and Exogenic reliance. The clarity of an organized presentation of facts or plans is only as powerful as the ability to pass that understanding on to others and connect in a way that is mutually enriching.

CHAPTER THIRTY

CONTROL

With Endogenic confidence, you do not need to know all the details

If you lead an organization and the executive you report to has concerns about your deliverables, does the executive approach you in the Endogenic state or the Exogenic state? In the Exogenic state, your executive will not seek to trust you but to take over and seek control. You will feel like you need to defend yourself as you are bombarded with a series of questions that chase down the content chain like a checklist. You feel micromanaged. Perhaps you even think that there is no reason or need for it.

It feels very different when a manager uses Endogenic confidence. In the Endogenic state, the questions do not feel like attacks. There is a connection between the person and all involved, like what we call team effort. Your manager connects with you, and you want to respond because you both want to get involved. You talk about the challenge and do not feel like you are the problem.

A person in the Exogenic state, when worried, wants data and control. A person in the Endogenic state, when worried, wants ideas and connection. The ideal leader knows when to draw on each.

For example, if you lead a highly technical group that is in charge of innovation, you know that you must build an empowered group. You let your coworkers own the parts they are responsible for, including the details, as you catalyze, facilitate, and orchestrate the parts. With Endogenic confidence, you do not need to know all the details. Your success will come from an informed exchange that enables all involved to create together. When control is needed, you can step in with that as well. If your manager relies only on Exogenic confidence, you may be viewed as lacking control. You will be expected to have all the answers. Even though you know your way is superior, you either need to show your manager that your way of empowerment is more effective or you need to provide what is expected.

CHAPTER THIRTY-ONE

CORPORATE CULTURE

It is commonly observed that as organizations grow, innovation slows

New companies are often driven by a culture that embraces Endogenic passion and inventiveness. As a company matures, its leaders tend to focus more and more on replicating, scaling, defining, and generating more profits, all under the pressure of time. Too often, this results in a gradual disregard for Endogenic qualities.

A corporate culture based on Exogenic reliance encourages behaviors like discipline, planning, control, conformity, consistency, and positional power. When an Exogenic culture dominates, leaders unknowingly promote and develop managers with the most dominant Exogenic states and management development opportunities only target further Exogenic growth. Innovators, vision-setters, and highly creative thinkers are less often promoted and disproportionately left out of the upper management ranks.

For talented innovators, this Exogenic mindset becomes impenetrable. Over time, Exogenic dominance forces many talented individuals to be overruled, dominated, left out of critical decisions, or driven out of the company. This is why it is commonly observed that as organizations grow, innovation slows. An Exogenic culture steadily dominates until leaders realize that the company has lost its spark and competitive edge.

Exogenic leaders prove themselves using data from the past. Their skill lies in gathering relevant data and compiling it into linear logic or proven facts that minimize fear in decision-making. This creates a highly structured and copy ready Exogenic culture that allows leaders to sustain what they have created and scale the results for greater profits. The consequence of an Exogenic culture is that leaders do not see what is new or missing.

On the other hand, leaders with strong Endogenic reliance operate with data that is in the making and has not yet become fact. These leaders can better withstand the pressure of fear and dedicate themselves to difficult challenges with curiosity, open-eyed exploration, understanding, and discovery, without depending on what has been proven or standardized before.

In order for fast-paced businesses to remain agile and innovative, they must embrace a culture that values Endogenic qualities such as openness, collaboration, connection, inventiveness, ambiguity, fearlessness, and vision. By encouraging a corporate culture that fosters Endogenic confidence, a company can manage the risks of Exogenic dominance.

No company has to choose to be either innovative and spontaneous or organized and productive. When leaders recognize the importance of both Endogenic and Exogenic reliance, they build a more balanced corporate culture that is better positioned for success.

A Balanced Corporate Culture	
Endogenic Reliance	**Exogenic Reliance**
Driven by discovery	Gap-driven
Intuitive	Mechanistic
Creative	Structured
Agile	Rigid
Unleashing potential	Fixing weakness
Clarity emerges	Clear plan developed
Spontaneous direction	Foreseeable direction

A Balanced Corporate Culture	
Endogenic Reliance	**Exogenic Reliance**
Interactional flow	Interactional protocol
Connection	Control
Collaboration	Direction
Invent	Copy
Bottom-up	Top-down
Follow curiosity	Follow expectation
Diversity	Conformity
Transforming	Clear beginning and end
Results are discernible	Results are measurable
Personal influence	Hierarchy
Self-reward	Threat and Reward
Win-win	Compromise
Seek meaning	Follow Rules
Passion	Discipline
Process	Goal
Vision	Plan
Synthesis	Analysis
Flexibility	Consistency

CHAPTER THIRTY-TWO

COVER-UPS

By being in your Endogenic state, you can see through a cover-up. All you have to do is to accept what you sensed, not what you were told

When a leader wants to exhibit lots of confidence but is not able to draw on Endogenic confidence, the only alternative is to compensate by forcefully displaying Exogenic confidence. The forcefulness makes others believe that this person is very confident. Exogenic confidence, when carefully implemented, can appear powerful without looking fake or rehearsed. This is a very common learned skill among leaders.

The problem that often surfaces when leaders lack Endogenic confidence is that they are not able to depend on their own sensing and feeling. For example, they often surprise themselves by making snappy comments, but they are quick to make cover-ups like, "I was just kidding" or "Don't be so sensitive" or "It was nothing." To build a reality without much Endogenic reliance, we must often forget, deny, or behave the opposite of what we feel. This often comes in the form of a cover-up.

People use cover-ups in an attempt to make their previous words or actions go away, but cover-ups do not change the way they felt at the time.

Most people do not know when they are hearing cover-ups. If someone says, "I was just kidding," people take that at face value and accept that what they heard was a joke.

By being in your Endogenic state, you can see through a cover-up. All you have to do is to accept what you sensed, not what you were told. If you hear a snappy comment while you are in your Endogenic state, you can sense if the person feels the way they say or is just making a joke.

Seeing cover-ups lets you see weaknesses and insecurities in others. You will change the amount of influence you let the other person have on you. It lets you see more of the whole individual and not be misguided by their skillful Exogenic ways.

CHAPTER THIRTY-THREE

ENTITLEMENT

Entitlement means you are relying on society and other people to make you feel strong

A common symptom of low Endogenic confidence is to behave entitled. Entitlement is a substitute for Endogenic fulfillment. Individuals lacking Endogenic confidence also lack fulfillment in life. They will seek fulfillment from outside of themselves in the form of gratification and rewards for their socially desired accomplishments, but no quantity of Exogenic accomplishments can create fulfillment.

If you ever catch yourself thinking you have earned certain rights or benefits that others ought to acknowledge and extend to you, that is a good moment to question why you believe that. Entitlement means you are relying on society and other people to make you feel strong. It means to pursue Exogenic satisfaction as opposed to Endogenic fulfillment.

Many highly successful people are chronically dissatisfied with life, even though they have made great accomplishments. When people live their lives driven by Exogenic dominance, they assume that what is missing in life must be outside of themselves. They seek to overcome gaps between what they have and what they perceive as better, believing that will make them happy and fulfilled in a way that can last. But the illusion pops over and over because Exogenic satisfaction demands accumulation and comparison.

Accumulation includes status related accomplishments like title, wealth, fame, or prestigious affiliations, as well as personal trophies or possessions used for image building. The value of each lies in our comparison to what we had before or to what others have now. When we see that we have accumulated more, we feel satisfaction but not fulfillment. Exogenic accumulations and comparisons only satisfy the Exogenic state. As soon as we reach one goal, we can only feel satisfied if we are working toward another.

The more we rely on Exogenic accumulation and comparison, the less we build Endogenic fulfillment. The long-term result is that we become under nurtured. This is the reason why some materialistically over-privileged people can behave very greedy and even more desperate to have more than someone who has much less. Their Exogenic dominance starves them from Endogenic fulfillment, which cannot be found through Exogenic achievements.

Extending this by decades, overly Exogenic individuals may accumulate many material things, but not an understanding of who they are. They start to behave entitled and expect to be compensated by society and other people, as if they were owed something. Without knowing, they are dependent on the environment for self-worth. They will not develop the wisdom and resources that lie within. They will not have deeply connected relationships or a rich appreciation of others. They will not truly understand the profundity of themselves, their spouse, or their children. They will end up concluding that fulfillment is a myth and their experience backs up what life is really like. They teach that to their children.

Everyone has some degree of hunger for fulfillment. The key is to realize that fulfillment comes through being in your Endogenic state. Accomplishments bring Exogenic satisfaction, but they can also bring fulfillment when we approach them with Endogenic reliance each step of the way. That takes noticing what is driving you. Do you pursue a goal because you feel a passion for it or because you assume it will bring you benefits or both? By aligning your goals with your curiosity and interests, you will build confidence that comes from inner strength, not just from outside achievements. The greatest achievement is to have significant success and feel very content. Life can be a fulfilling process including accomplishments that are rich with heartwarming stories and fulfillment that empowers development of the self. With fulfillment, entitled behavior fades away.

CHAPTER THIRTY-FOUR

ENVY

Highly Exogenic workers sacrificed much joy to accomplish what they have in life, and to accept that there could have been an easier way or a shortcut makes them think they were cheated

A symptom of low Endogenic reliance is envy. For example, people who work hard in the Exogenic state (with discipline, control, plans, or against their desire) feel betrayed when they observe that ease, passion, and fun of Endogenic reliance has a greater return. They might be very irritated when a coworker—who seems to jump from one idea to the next without sticking to established processes and structures—suddenly gets extra funding, a promotion, or lots of praise for implementing a new initiative or landing an important contract.

The hard worker who over-relies on trusting the Exogenic state is prone to criticize the ways of the Endogenic state. They see ease and call it laziness or dumb luck. Highly Exogenic workers sacrificed much joy to accomplish what they have in life, and to accept that there could have been an easier way or a shortcut makes them think they were cheated. To avoid this pain and humiliation, they may deny that there can be another way. They will believe that everyone should take the long path and will find satisfaction in making others believe that there is only one way. These views are the result of envy, and denying the envy makes trust in the Exogenic state even stronger.

A person lacking Endogenic reliance is deprived of the resources of the Endogenic state and can only follow the learned path. This becomes especially problematic with, for example, a leader of a division that needs to be open to change, a teacher who has power over students with potential for brilliance, or caretakers of children who have more Endogenic reliance than they do.

CHAPTER THIRTY-FIVE

EXECUTIVE COACHING

When a company wants to develop the greatest potential of its leaders,
it is important to make a distinction between developing Endogenic
versus Exogenic reliance

To compete globally, companies must leverage their talent by providing resources to those who advance the company's innovation and vision the most. In recent years, companies have turned to executive coaching to address this need.

Executive coaching brings the promise of advancing all forms of management development, from fixing problematic behavior to unleashing the potential of the brightest leaders. It is currently the fastest growing professional service for management and leadership development. The International Coach Federation defines executive coaching as: "Partnering with clients in a thought-provoking and creative process that inspires them to maximize their personal and professional potential." Ultimately, coaching is meant to advance the competitive success of an organization.

The predominant methodology used by executive coaches today is based on cognitive and behavioral psychological schools of thought that result in Exogenic learning for participants. Coaches gather stakeholder input about the client, perform gap analyses, write development plans, set improvement goals, and modify the client's behavior to meet the expectations of others. When a person follows instructions, undergoes training, or acquires prescribed skills, the process is Exogenic.

Exogenic learning tools appear powerful. Surveys, questionnaires, and stakeholder interviews provide a synopsis of the personality traits, strengths, and weaknesses of the client. Clients learn how others perceive them and can consider changing those perceptions by demonstrating targeted situational or generic behavioral changes.

Exogenic learning provides a fast route to identifying and replicating the behaviors, procedural knowledge, and methodologies that make a leader look, think, and act the way other successful leaders look, think, and act. By focusing on behavioral modification, executive coaches help future leaders quickly develop Exogenic confidence (looking confident), Exogenic authority (exerting positional authority), Exogenic productivity (replicating and scaling), and Exogenic identity (I am defined by others). Exogenic learning is a quick way to boost leadership capabilities to the level of the norm.

Most coaches promise they will help executives become smarter, more strategic, better at leading, and able to advance faster. These ambitious goals cannot be accomplished through Exogenic learning alone. Coaching may be presented as a customized facilitation process for senior leaders, but with an Exogenic design, it is limited to being a controlling and conforming tool that trains leaders to change their behavior.

When a company wants to develop the greatest potential of its leaders, it is important to make a distinction between developing Endogenic versus Exogenic reliance. Becoming a great leader always takes both Endogenic and Exogenic development. If Endogenic development is ignored or discredited, leadership development will be limited to replicating what has been successful in the past and a company will lose its creative edge.

Many human resource professionals and company executives are not aware of the underlying methodology that coaching brings to an organization, nor are they familiar with the impact this methodology has on the corporate culture and organizational health. What this means for the organization is that executive coaching is advancing the already-established corporate culture of Exogenic reliance, which encourages behaviors like compromise, control, conformity, and positional authority.

Leaders who respond most favorably to Exogenic learning are those who are at the beginning of the long journey to becoming thought leaders, vision-setters, or innovators for the company. Without a strong Exogenic base, a leader is not taken seriously by others and is at a disadvantage regarding navigating the established procedures and meeting expectations of others. Executive coaching can provide a personalized process for advancing these skills.

Once essential management knowledge has been acquired, adding even more Exogenic dominance becomes counterproductive. The more leaders become conditioned to solve problems and lead others with Exogenic dominance, the less they are able to break through their default state to draw upon Endogenic power. Exogenic dominance is a hindrance to creative and insightful leadership.

Whereas Exogenic learning provides the tools, knowledge, and best-known methods for molding someone into becoming a better leader, Endogenic learning enables individuals to grow their unique and authentic leadership potential in a way that unleashes creativity, vision, and charisma. With Endogenic reliance comes greater Endogenic confidence (feeling confident) Endogenic authority (having personal influence), Endogenic productivity (innovation), and Endogenic identity (self-definition). Once a person has developed a strong Exogenic state, the greatest growth potential lies in advancing Endogenic reliance. Leaders with strong Endogenic reliance become the vision-setters and inspiring leaders of a company.

Executive Coaching for Leadership Development		
Development	Endogenic	Exogenic
Confidence	Feeling confident	Looking confident
Authority	Personal influence	Positional authority
Productivity	Innovate	Replicate/Scale
Identity	Self-defined	Defined by others

The failure of executive coaching is most noticed by the talented and gifted. Highly ambitious and talented leaders seek to unfold everything that is possible in life. They strive for more than Exogenic learning and behavioral modification. These individuals resist overly dominant Exogenic learning because it seems like busywork or a waste of time. Once they have tried working with an executive coach who instructs them about what to do, the most talented and gifted individuals often decline continuing. They are not looking for instructions. The next-generation leader wants to pioneer ahead of expectations. They seek to unleash what they sense must be inside them. That requires innovation, not adaptation. It means to excel, not fit in.

Many highly talented senior managers and executives feel they have to hide their ambivalence to company-sponsored coaching or their actions will be misinterpreted as not wanting to advance or resisting feedback from others. This leaves highly valuable leaders in a company without resources for advancing their growth, other than learning from experience and continuing to invent themselves.

Executive coaching could be an ideal way for leaders to experience building Endogenic reliance. Rather than providing Exogenic tools such as peer surveys, checklists, or assignments, this new form of coaching would establish a client-driven process, where the executive sets the agenda and methods vary according to the situation. In a one-on-one, face-to-face setting, both Endogenic and Exogenic needs could be addressed. This new form of "Duogenic coaching" would be based on real problems of the present. The coach would help the executive directly resolve business challenges through strategic, responsive, and proactive approaches.

This kind of coaching session cannot be preplanned. When the leader is describing a pressing challenge, an astute observer can notice when words become mechanical or lack emotional connection. A Duogenic coach would be able to point out moments when Endogenic is more effective than Exogenic. The coach could help the executive learn to break the mold of an overpowering Exogenic state by reminding the executive to draw on Endogenic reliance at the right moment, in order to reflect on the complexities of the problem at hand.

In the Endogenic state, you can connect missing links, empathize, sense tension, and navigate through conflicts. You access your Endogenic state when you want the ability to capture a reality of greater scope and complexity. You switch back to Exogenic to summarize and analyze. You would learn to use, switch, and leverage both states.

When we are stuck on a difficult challenge, it is usually because one state dominates the other, preventing progress without us knowing. Having access to both states allows you to experience clarity. This lays the groundwork for seeing new possibilities and approaches that were not visible before and could not have occurred before. You experience inspiration and insight. Solutions come to you for problems you thought were hopeless. Nothing you discover in your Endogenic state will surprise you because it all makes sense. You may wonder why you did not recognize the solution before.

Experiencing the choice between Endogenic and Exogenic power will make you feel better and stronger. When you solve a challenge this way, you are energized, and you will immediately begin to act on what you discovered. You will see a clear path. You may even exhibit a new behavior, but your change is a self-chosen reconfiguration.

Every individual has different development needs. Some will benefit most from Exogenic learning and others from Endogenic learning. As soon as the executive coaching industry understands the core of this duality, the opportunity to improve becomes clear. With an understanding of Endogenic and Exogenic reliance, executives, human resource professionals, and coaches can consider a more effective approach to organizational and leadership advancement.

CHAPTER THIRTY-SIX

FEAR

When we see Endogenic reliance applied in extreme situations, we may call it heroic or great leadership

Fear is the biggest hindrance to becoming a Duogenic leader. When we have fear, we easily subordinate ourselves to Exogenic dominance and become followers of rules and previous learning. When the fear level is high, we do not dare to try something new. We stay alert and are afraid of relaxing or calming down. We focus on our goal of becoming safe, as we stay ready to fight and defend. Fear captivates us. The greater the fear, the less the chance that we can break lose.

If we do not know to choose between Endogenic and Exogenic, we end up in our default mode. It takes intentional will and a high level of Endogenic reliance to break away from the Exogenic state when fear dominates. The greater the fear, the more challenging it is to switch to the Endogenic state.

Facing fear as a Duogenic leader means that you are able to choose between your Endogenic and Exogenic state. In the Endogenic state, you experience the moment in full in such a way that you can actually steer the moment.

In the Endogenic state, time seems to be slower. When a crisis occurs, you have time to see the situation unfold in every detail and intervene in a way you intentionally select. Others around you, in their Exogenic states, appear frozen and helpless as you take action to save a life, avoid an injury, or silence an aggressor with perfectly chosen words. When we see Endogenic reliance applied in extreme situations, we may call it heroic or great leadership.

Approaching a challenge in the Endogenic state allows you to explore the challenge, connect to the parts, sense, feel, gauge, and intuit until you get it.

Fear is pervasive in many work environments. As a result, most people have to rely on the Exogenic state most of the time. That is the main reason that we do not have more stellar performances at work, on stage, in meeting rooms, or in daily interactions.

Chapter Thirty-Seven

Female Executives

With strong Endogenic reliance you more easily retain your own unique perceptions

Women have an untapped advantage in business. During childhood, due to the customs of society, girls are often encouraged more than boys to appreciate their Endogenic qualities like having feelings, imagination, or deep connections with friends. They are also less likely to be pushed into Exogenic dominance such as being tough, disregarding sensations, or winning at all costs. The outcome is that Endogenic reliance is more prevalent among women than men.

Regardless of gender, with strong Endogenic reliance you more easily retain your own unique perceptions. Unique perceptions are the basis for creativity, passion, intrinsic motivation, and a sense of independence. People with less Endogenic reliance have less capacity to welcome their perceptions and they become more obedient, conforming, and dependent on confirmation from outside. In the workplace, Endogenic reliance translates into the ability to lead in new directions, invent new products, inspire others, and have contagious passion and drive. These are the qualities many companies seek for executive leadership.

This advantage is only theoretical because it does not play out in the workplace. What happens is that in our Exogenic world, overly Exogenic individuals misread Endogenic reliance as the absence of expected Exogenic behaviors. A person who exhibits Endogenic qualities such as compassion, connection, spontaneity, vision, curiosity, or contemplation appears to lack the outward ambition, intent, or fighting instinct the Exogenic leaders think is needed. Individuals who rely more on their Endogenic state than the norm tend to be misunderstood.

For example, when a female worker responds to an aggressive accusation by being calm and seeking to clarify what her accuser is trying to say, her overly Exogenic manager may interpret that behavior as weak, thinking she did not have the courage to fight back or defend herself with the same vigor as her accuser. The manager is only able to think in Exogenic terms, which are often limited to believing there is a right and a wrong way to respond to personal attacks.

The dynamic that plays out at work is that people with strong Endogenic reliance usually drop their Endogenic ways when they are confronted with too much Exogenic behavior. They do not make use of their Endogenic strength. Worse, however, is that these people end up with greater frustration at work. A person with strong Endogenic reliance will notice when their Endogenic state is overruled by others. They are less tolerant of Exogenic dominance and suffer the most in environments that are dominantly Exogenic. This wears on them and robs them of energy that they could be using for greater accomplishments.

People with strong Endogenic reliance often end up adapting trustingly to the Exogenic behavior of their company. They do not know that fitting in may actually be inhibiting their potential. Women are advised to exhibit more Exogenic traits and fewer Endogenic traits to keep up with the Exogenic world. They reduce their personal power by suppressing the Endogenic state. Even the most gifted, talented, creative, and innovative leaders are affected.

Some individuals have discovered how to capitalize on their advantage of already having more Endogenic strength. Rather than giving in to the Exogenic dominance, they have learned to educate those around them to better understand and appreciate their opposing approach.

When a company can embrace a new culture that supports both Endogenic and Exogenic reliance and especially seeks out Duogenic leaders, a surge of creative force and innovation will occur. It will be important for women leaders to be part of this change. They could have an easier time leading the change and may be the most motivated to see it happen.

CHAPTER THIRTY-EIGHT

FREEZING A FEELING

An Exogenic feeling is like a frozen copy of the original

Freezing a feeling is the act of converting Endogenic sensing and feeling into an Exogenic feeling. When a strong feeling occurs, such as intense joy, love, or tenderness, a person with low Endogenic reliance is unknowingly seduced to preserve or freeze the feeling in hopes it will not go away. At that moment, the Endogenic state is rejected and replaced by the Exogenic memory or idea of the feeling.

For example, if you have a strong Endogenic emotion, like happiness, you may not notice exactly when that emotion fades away, and you may be shocked when you realize it is almost gone. If you wish for it to last, you may try to hold on to the happiness by freezing it. At that moment, you reject the Endogenic state and now rely on the Exogenic idea of being happy. You may reinforce it by thinking you should be happy and that you should stop doubting. That is very different from the actual feeling of being happy.

People are seduced into creating Exogenic feelings because the Endogenic state is often fleeting. With low Endogenic reliance, we think we are shortchanged when a nice feeling suddenly goes away. Only those with strong Endogenic reliance have the confidence to allow very good feelings to vanish.

When we freeze a feeling, thought, or behavior, we give up the chance for newness, spontaneity, and discovery. We hang on to a memory, trying to relive it. The greater value may be in what we could have now, not in what we froze. The new Exogenic feeling is disconnected from the source that fueled the original feeling. An Exogenic feeling is like a frozen copy of the original.

To freeze a feeling, one merely has to switch to the Exogenic state by recalling or acting out what the original feeling was like. It is as simple as thinking you should be happy or deciding you should have the same enthusiasm you had before. By repeating the thoughts and actions that an original feeling evoked, we recreate or extend the feeling while in the Exogenic state.

A common way to observe freezing a feeling is in a group situation where you might be with coworkers having fun, joking or exchanging some entertaining thoughts. After some time passes, you might notice that one of the members of your group is laughing at odd moments or seems to have overly enthusiastic facial expressions. That is a sign that this person is now recreating what was felt earlier. The feeling is now Exogenic and is being acted out instead of felt.

Overly Exogenic individuals will usually not know the difference between feeling an Endogenic feeling and hanging on to the memory and idea of that feeling. They will just tell themselves that they are having fun (or are happy, or are in love). The problem with this lack of Endogenic reliance is that we build illusions about ourselves and become more artificial, less spontaneous, less open, and less capable of connecting with others through meaningful and genuine exchanges.

We do not only freeze happy and positive feelings. Hurtful and dramatic events undergo the same pattern when our Exogenic state overpowers living in the present. For example, someone may resent another person based on a bad experience with this person. By keeping the feeling as an Exogenic feeling, they will continue to resent the person irrespective of any changes the other may have undergone. The more we allow Exogenic reliance to dominate over Endogenic reliance, the more we carry our past with us and the less we are open to change and current realities.

You can interrupt this pattern by simply pausing and noticing what you feel, not what you should feel. This will bring you back to your Endogenic state, help balance your Endogenic and Exogenic states, and experience reality instead of building illusions.

CHAPTER THIRTY-NINE

FULFILLMENT

Overly Exogenic goal orientation wipes out any sense of "I want to"
and leaves you with "I have to." You are never done

Successful people who lack Endogenic confidence also lack the feeling of fulfillment. Most talented and accomplished people believe that the driving force behind their success is the constant pursuit of goals. They feel they have come so far because they have not relaxed yet. These individuals are focusing only on building Exogenic confidence. Unfortunately, the more successful they become, the more ambivalent they feel about the value of their success because of the enslaving dynamic that over-reliance on Exogenic confidence causes.

Goals are Exogenic. When a target is set, it lies ahead of us as a gain to be achieved. While it is a fiction, it gives the promise of improving, increasing, and getting ahead. When a goal is reached, it becomes the new standard that we compare against. To improve and increase again, we set a new, higher goal. With expectation, commitment, structure, and discipline, we push with Exogenic confidence to reach goal after goal. Once you get in the habit of making achievements in the Exogenic state, you easily lose sight of the option to achieve the Endogenic way. You disconnect from the longings that draw you to what fills you with passion.

Goals can feel like tunnels that you need to go through to come out the other end. Focusing on the tunnel, you lose track of what is happening outside the tunnel. This disciplined focus robs you of many daily choices. Overly Exogenic goal orientation wipes out any sense of "I want to" and leaves you with "I have to." You are never done. As soon as one hurdle is overcome, you set your eyes on the next one. Not relying on your Endogenic state, you cannot deeply relax. You lose sight of knowing when you end with one goal and start on a new one. It all looks like the same steep climb ahead. You have a hard time knowing when you are done for now and when to truly celebrate. The Exogenic state has pushed your Endogenic cues of enjoyment, accomplishment, and satisfaction out of reach and it dominates by dangling more goals in front of your eyes instead.

Eventually, individuals who neglect their Endogenic state will begin to resent that all their hard work does not also bring meaning, satisfaction, and fulfillment. As we make achievements and earn society's rewards through Exogenic reliance, the earnings do not nurture our starving Endogenic state.

Without knowing better, this cycle gets worse. The more we resent our lack of fulfillment, the more we cling to our Exogenic reliance by placing more goals and demands on ourselves. The resentment may eventually turn into anger against the self that first manifests with the thought of "I'm not good enough." Later that anger leads to insecurity and severely limits an individual's potential for success. Many highly competent professionals are used to thinking they are not good enough. Whatever they do, it is always less than they feel they should have done.

By strengthening Endogenic reliance, you can pursue goals, accomplish more, have passion, and be fulfilled. With both forms of reliance, you can feel satisfaction and fulfillment while you chase goals. Fulfillment becomes available to you every moment instead of only after some far off fiction or longing. You do not need to wait until someday, like after you have gotten a better job or saved more money or gained more respect.

One way to get started is to frequently remind yourself to explore. In the middle of focusing intently on a goal, just ask yourself some questions: What is important to me right now? Does what I am in the midst of doing make sense? Do I like myself right now? Am I aware of what is going on around me? Have I taken a deep breath lately? Can I make this moment nicer for me? As you experience your Endogenic state, fulfillment comes from the moment. Only in the Endogenic state can you have insights, new ideas, or revelations. Suddenly, you may have an idea that completely trumps the goal you were so intently working on. Or maybe you will decide to take a break and go on a walk. The more frequently you access your Endogenic state, the less enslaved and more fulfilled you will be.

CHAPTER FORTY

GOALS

With Exogenic reliance, we pursue goals. With Endogenic reliance, we engage in pathfinding

When expectations are high and much is at stake, we are trained to fixate on a goal. Keeping a goal in mind leads us in the right direction, but we also need to be aware of each moment so we can respond appropriately to the challenges on the path. As simple as that concept sounds, it is very challenging to live by. With Exogenic reliance, we pursue goals. With Endogenic reliance, we engage in pathfinding. A Duogenic leader freely does both.

Duogenic leaders are often misunderstood by majorities. They are capable of abandoning Exogenic pursuits and switching to Endogenic pathfinding and vice versa. In doing so, they sometimes change the goal they defined earlier. With pathfinding, they are able to discover a new or revised goal that is better than the original one. Critics who follow Exogenic measurements may say, at the time, that the leader has failed. Those who see the bigger picture know it was a breakthrough.

A goal should be adjusted when reality changes. However, if Exogenic fixation on the goal will not allow for change, then either the goal will not be reached or it will be reached and still be a failure. Fixation on goals has the effect of not letting us be in tune with the moment, which makes us miss hints and data points needed for steering.

By defining "goal" differently, with balanced Endogenic and Exogenic reliance, you can choose a path that not only has reward in its achievement but you also learn and grow each step along the way. The path needs to have appeal in itself, not just as a means to the goal. By connecting to the path in emotion, cognition, and behavior, the goal and the path will reinforce each other in synergy. As you pursue the goal, you also note many curious moments on the path, and you recognize the smallest quantities of progress that are due to your influence. In the end, there is either double gain or single gain. The path has enriched you even if the goal could not.

CHAPTER FORTY-ONE

HEAR YOURSELF

If you can remember to switch to your Endogenic state, even for just a moment, you can hear yourself speak

When you are in the Endogenic state, you can hear yourself as you speak. You can notice your emotions as you communicate with others, know what your body language expresses, and be aware of what signals you send with the sound of your voice. With Endogenic self-awareness, you have the agility to steer your expression and impact at any moment. It is a humbling and powerful way to exist. To embrace yourself this way leads to fewer misinterpretations by others, and by understanding yourself, you better understand others.

Many people do not hear themselves speak. In fact, many do not really know what their own voice sounds like. What if an executive wanted to advance himself but did not realize that his voice was limiting his ability to influence others? He would probably know that speaking was not his strong suit, but may not be sure why. He might have assumed he was born with a somewhat weak voice and there was not much he could do about it. Chances are that even though he knows what words he says, he does not know what his voice sounds like.

A sharp, whiny, soft, monotonous, or grumpy voice has a big effect on how others interpret important messages. Many people use entirely different voices, situationally, without realizing it. In relaxed situations, a person might have a calm, strong, and clear voice, but under stress in a room with coworkers, the tone may change to being sharp or nervous.

It is very difficult to be on output (speaking, acting, etc.) and input (sensing and feeling) at the same time. It is only possible when you are in the Endogenic state or when you can nimbly switch back and forth between your Endogenic and Exogenic states. Exogenic self-awareness is not awareness in the moment. It is a critique of what occurred in the past or what should be in the future. We are in the Exogenic state when we deliver a prepared message, perform to a script, give instructions, or direct others, but we need to be in the Endogenic state to have Endogenic self-awareness, which lets us experience the moment as it unfolds.

To influence what the moment holds, we need to apply ad hoc what the moment needs, for example, supporting the delivery of our statements with a strong voice. To know what the moment needs while we perform a prepared task demands that we move back and forth between the Endogenic and Exogenic state. Being able to accomplish both output and input requires the ability for both states to work hand in hand, allowing you to hear yourself when speaking to others, especially in challenging situations. If you can remember to switch to your Endogenic state, even for just a moment, you can hear yourself speak, and adjust your volume, articulation, or intonation.

It takes curiosity to attempt hearing yourself speak. As small moments accumulate, you gain knowledge and empowerment. Your ability to deliver a prepared message (Exogenic) and take part in the moment (Endogenic) reveals insight into how you deliver your words and it opens space for you to observe others to see if and how your message is being received.

When you are in a meeting and you know you have to perform, whether that is leading the meeting, voicing your opinion, or influencing an outcome, do you observe how you are affecting others while you are performing? If you ask company leaders this question, some will know and most will have no idea. Those who have never observed and performed at the same time may find it curious and decide to try it. By mastering Endogenic self-awareness while performing, a wealth of new information is available for increasing one's effectiveness.

To observe while performing means you not only hear yourself as you speak, but you also notice your emotions, whom you are speaking to, and how everyone in the room interacts with you and with each other. When you are able to observe your impact on others, you start to see who responds to you and how. You will notice both verbal and nonverbal cues. You will pick up on where others stand in their agreement or disagreement with you. You will know who has bought into what you say, who respects you more or less, and who affirms your role or not.

Some of what you always wished you could know is laid out right before your eyes. You might notice that a person who was ignorant of your charter, and pretty useless as an ally in the past, is now thinking about what you just said and listening intently. You may see that you had misjudged this person and you may find satisfaction in knowing that you can go further with this person than you thought. Suddenly, someone who you assumed was difficult to deal with could be on your side.

As you look around more while you are addressing the group, you can see who wants to fight you, who is getting bored, and who is interested.

To observe while performing is a very advanced application of Duogenic leadership. It may take years to master, but it holds tremendous returns. With it you can fully steer your leadership path, increase your performance and impact on others, customize your contribution to the situation's needs, and discover possibilities that you could not see before.

CHAPTER FORTY-TWO

ILLUSION

In the Exogenic state, we act as if we are the makers of reality

Lack of Endogenic reliance breeds illusion. One of the great risks about our fear of the Endogenic state is our desire to deny our Endogenic state. We try to freeze things or keep them unchanged. For example, rather than acknowledge that a relationship is deteriorating or that we are feeling less aligned with an important stakeholder at work, we may avoid the Endogenic thought and try to believe that nothing of relevance has changed. Regardless of how hard we try to freeze reality, it changes anyway. Exogenic beliefs help us build an illusion. When we rely on an illusion, we forget the original emotion or the threatening thought. If we cling strongly to such illusions, we do not even notice when a very significant change has occurred.

To keep up our illusions, we cling to the Exogenic state and fear change. In our Exogenic state, we can accept linear newness but not disruptive novelty. Our Exogenic state cannot deal with undefined circumstances. When we are in the Exogenic state, the only way we can integrate something new into our life is for the new to be a scaled or extended version of the old. It has to be safely derived from what we already accept. When we do not let our Endogenic state engage, we are not equipped to deal with a disruption and gap between old and new; the prospect holds too little information to bear the fear of the unknown.

Living predominantly in the Exogenic state easily turns into a cage. Our illusion of reality is self-limiting. When we have a feeling or dream we do not like, we call it random and dismiss it. We behave as though what we dismissed does not exist. In the Exogenic state, we act as if we are the makers of reality. It is comforting, but it stifles the new horizons that our Endogenic state can provide. We trivialize the Endogenic state's thoughts and feelings and subordinate them to our opinion. We behave as if we were above the Endogenic state when in fact the Endogenic state is our source for all that is new, and we are rejecting it.

We are attracted to illusion when it is more desirable than reality. This is seen every day at social gatherings full of small talk and dramatized enthusiasm or amongst people where everyone is trying to impress each other. The collective Exogenic state gives the impression that the people in the group are more connected to each other than they really are. When we are in the Exogenic state and expose ourselves to others in their Exogenic states, we can lose ourselves. We get carried away by participating in a collective Exogenic state.

If you were in your Exogenic state when you looked at such a group, you might interpret that there is a lot of bonding going on. You may even get jealous over what you believe to see. In the Endogenic state, however, an observer does not see bonding and in fact sees plenty of space to step in with an engaging question or statement. A person with strong Endogenic reliance can easily slip into their Endogenic state and break the spell of chitchat. Others will either reject this and see it as an intrusion (if they have very weak Endogenic reliance), or they may respond in their Endogenic state too, transforming the entire mood of the interaction. In the Endogenic state, keeping up an illusion is not an option.

In nearly every profession, people default to illusions. Unfortunately, this can lead to serious errors, such as a wrong medical diagnosis or rejecting a creative business idea. Lack of Endogenic reliance makes it difficult for us to be in touch with the needs of the moment. We only feel comfortable relying on already-established facts. We end up doing everything by the book and not using our Endogenic intelligence, giving up capabilities such as intuitive risk assessment, inspiration, and creativity.

We are better served by choosing which state we want to be in instead of merely defaulting to Exogenic reliance. For example, it can be very beneficial to take an Exogenic leap of faith by making a decision with no intuitive reference. We can choose to rely on what has worked in the past, and that can be a good choice. However, by not developing Endogenic reliance, we are forced into over-reliance on the Exogenic state, so the option of choice is gone.

To avoid building illusions, we need to respond to our Endogenic thoughts and feelings instead of brushing them off. We should frequently question ourselves about what we experience with thoughts like "This is odd" or "That doesn't match what I know about myself" or "Should I consider this?" It takes curiosity. When we fully embrace freedom of thinking, sensing, and feeling and do not deny and dismiss what does not fit, we build our Endogenic reliance and uncover a more realistic picture of life.

Chapter Forty-Three

Innovation

*Exogenic dominance, coupled with a lack of Endogenic reliance among
leaders, is what stifles innovation and creativity in an organization*

All innovation comes from being in the Endogenic state. There is
no other way to innovate. The more a company can nurture and
support Endogenic reliance on all levels and balance it with
Exogenic reliance, the more innovation and creativity will unfold.

Many large, well-established companies tend to promote highly
Exogenic leaders more than highly Endogenic leaders. As a
result, the top leaders in many older companies severely lack
Endogenic confidence. The leaders in these companies rely on
their Exogenic states because that is what was rewarded over
time.

This culture of Exogenic dominance grows on itself to the point
where most top managers do not know how to build Endogenic
strength in the workforce and, in fact, they strongly discourage
Endogenic reliance among their direct reports and peers.
Exogenic dominance, coupled with a lack of Endogenic reliance
among leaders, is what stifles innovation and creativity in an
organization.

When a highly Exogenic organization wants to encourage
innovation and creativity, Exogenic decision makers look for
Exogenic systems that are proven to encourage innovation.
Exogenic systems, however, do not solve the lack of Endogenic
development. The company dedicates more and more Exogenic
resources to encourage innovation, but while employees become
fluent in the language of inventiveness and collaboration, the
root factor for encouraging innovation is not addressed.

Exogenic leaders who want to support the most creative vision
setters in an organization can start by getting out of the way.

Individuals with strong Endogenic reliance are in a minority position. When they are forced to battle against majority beliefs to advance their creative vision, too much of their effort goes into fighting for legitimacy and swimming against the tide instead of driving the disruptive pathways of innovation.

To best support innovation and creativity, leaders should gain Duogenic qualities. Duogenic leaders understand that Endogenic and Exogenic reliance each has its place. They are best able to orchestrate collaboration between Endogenic and Exogenic talent. When competent, strong Endogenic innovators have support and protection from Exogenic dominance, they can channel time and energy into architecting the new instead of fighting against a wall of structure and rigidity.

Innovation in an organization requires a culture that embraces Endogenic qualities. There must be a balance between Endogenic and Exogenic so that Exogenic constraints such as long-term planning, deadlines, procedures, protocols, schedules, and interpersonal formalities do not overpower Endogenic qualities that support innovation such as curiosity, passion, discovery, accuracy, unpredictability, and spontaneity. A balanced environment, where Endogenic qualities are respected and understood, will attract, retain, and encourage more leaders with Endogenic power, resulting in a more innovative culture.

CHAPTER FORTY-FOUR

INTERVENTION

*For an Exogenic environment to transform, it must first break down
or implode*

When managers perform primarily in the Exogenic state, success is measured by hitting or missing a goal. Therefore, it takes failure before Exogenic leadership allows for course correction.

In the Exogenic state, we follow plans until they fail us. We rely on learned knowledge until the outcome is not as expected. We focus on our goal and then draw conclusions after the fact. If achieving a goal looks more difficult than we anticipated, we dedicate more time or allocate more people instead of questioning the goal or the assumptions behind it. The Exogenic response to a failing plan is to add more Exogenic tools, like more planning, more checking, more analyzing, more data processing, or more people. We depend on our plans and the promise those plans hold. When the promise starts to slip, we intensify our investment in the plan we already have.

On the other hand, Endogenic intervention allows a leader to let go of assumptions and be open to discovery. In the Endogenic state, a leader can discern and contemplate, bringing to the surface what might have been overlooked, unexpected, unknown, or unprepared for. In the Endogenic state, we sense, feel, ponder, and come to ask the right questions before we take action. Managers who are capable of both Endogenic and Exogenic leadership can shift swiftly between the Endogenic and Exogenic states. They do not need to hit a wall to sense a wall. They do not need the threat of losing everything in order to change course, question assumptions, re-prioritize goals, or know when to give up.

When a management environment is overly Exogenic, it cannot easily transform or bend with changing markets and needs. For an Exogenic environment to transform, it must first break down or implode. Far better is to begin an intervention by seeking the guidance of individuals with strong Endogenic reliance. On occasion, an individual or group with strong Endogenic and Exogenic reliance will gain the respect of top leadership and lead an Endogenic transformation long before everything crashes. These individuals can see the urgency ahead of others and it is blindingly obvious to them that a change must occur.

Once Exogenic dominance breaks down and people with Endogenic reliance are allowed to take the lead, the transformation that follows can be like a phoenix rising out of the ashes. Unfortunately, Endogenic interventions are usually only attempted after a miserable failure, total collapse, or at the latest hour when disaster seems inevitable.

Why do we use Endogenic interventions so late in the game? People do not readily give up their overpowering Exogenic reign. Exogenic dominance in an organization usually intensifies over time. Even though management knows the importance of having diverse ideas, independence of decision-making, freedom to experiment, and the courage to question or circumvent bureaucracy, integrating and promoting Endogenic strength in an organization does not make it high on the urgency list when leaders believe the system is not broken. Through overuse of the Exogenic state and rejection and condemnation of the Endogenic state, overly Exogenic leaders are putting their organizations at risk.

CHAPTER FORTY-FIVE

LIMITS OF EXOGENIC RELIANCE

*In the Endogenic state, sensations and feelings reveal data that
Exogenic thoughts cannot*

When you approach a difficult challenge, but mostly with Exogenic reliance, there may be a point at which you reach the end of your thinking capacity. You can recognize the limits of Exogenic reliance by noticing when your thoughts start to go in loops. You may find that you cannot let go of a certain idea, analyzing more does not bring more clarity, your options seem too complex, no solution seems right, or your progress has stopped.

Once we exhaust the situational capacity of the Exogenic state, further progress comes from sensing, feeling, and engaging in the moment. By switching to the Endogenic state, we immerse in an experience instead of clinging to previous thoughts. In the Endogenic state, sensations and feelings reveal data that Exogenic thoughts cannot.

Below are some examples of when Exogenic reliance has reached its limit. To get beyond these points, you can switch from Exogenic to Endogenic:

- when your thinking repeats in circles
- when your progress stagnates
- when you do not know what to do
- when you do not know what to think
- when advice from others is not helping
- when analyzing is not bringing in new data

- when you are stuck
- when you are looking for progress that you cannot exactly define
- when you want a way out but do not see any options
- when you have contradictory ideas
- when you need to decide but there are too many options
- when you are anxious
- when you cannot change course because you have invested too much
- when you need to escape the iron fist of control
- when you cannot understand
- when you are in conflict
- when you are confused
- when you hear mixed messages
- when you are overwhelmed
- when you are defensive

To solve difficult challenges, we usually start with Exogenic analysis and thought. We gather information, consider all the options, and make decisions based on the knowledge we have. Full intelligence, however, must include drawing from the Endogenic state. If you attempt to solve a difficult challenge without any Endogenic reliance, you will find yourself analyzing to the hundredth degree. At some point, you will stop advancing intellectually on the problem. This kind of Exogenic analysis is fueled by fear of the Endogenic state. It is obsessive in nature and does not result in wise or insightful decisions. When thought becomes obsessive, it is an indicator that you have reached the limits of what Exogenic reliance can do for you. It serves as a reminder to switch to the Endogenic state for progress.

CHAPTER FORTY-SIX

LONGING

*Most people attempt to fix Endogenic longings by making them go
away with Exogenic distractions*

Endogenic longing is an urge or plea for Endogenic fulfillment.
In order to fully unfold psychologically, we must develop and
balance both Endogenic and Exogenic reliance. By neglecting our
Endogenic state and continuously overpowering it with Exogenic
goals, actions, and distractions, we develop a longing for
Endogenic fulfillment. Chronic overpowering of the Endogenic
state starves the self of Endogenic meaning and fulfillment.
Endogenic fulfillment requires sensing and feeling our desires,
passions, frustrations, or hurts and nurturing the self.

In the Exogenic state, Endogenic longings are misinterpreted.
Instead of sensing and feeling the Endogenic message, we only
notice an unwanted restlessness, void, or emptiness. Most people
attempt to fix Endogenic longings by making them go away with
Exogenic distractions like getting busy, pursuing a goal, working
late, taking on a new chore, being around others, talking,
shopping, watching television, turning on music, eating, or
drinking—anything that makes the uncomfortable feeling go
away or be forgotten.

Any Exogenic response to an Endogenic longing is merely a
substitution that leaves the longing for Endogenic fulfillment
unsatisfied. For example, by never addressing your lack of
confidence at work, you may build Endogenic longing, but in the
Exogenic state, you may only notice that you are burned out or
sharp tempered. That uncomfortable state will go away as soon as
you find a distraction, like watching television or going to a bar
with friends. Although substitutions do not address the
underlying longing, they do let us temporarily dismiss the signals
that surfaced. Substitutions are a quick fix for the psychologically

unaware. Responding to Endogenic longings with substitutions is like feeding a hole that never seems to fill. The longing always comes back and more distractions are needed.

If you could instead be in your Endogenic state, you would feel the driving force of Endogenic longing, whether it be loneliness, anger, desire, hurt, anxiety, stress, love, or the need for comfort. With this knowledge, you can choose to satisfy your Endogenic needs and use Duogenic strength to help figure out what to do under the circumstances. For example, if your confidence has been shaken by repeated criticisms from your boss, you would notice that you feel hurt and you could explore how your own opinion of yourself compares to what your manager told you. You might realize something you want to say to your manager or it might dawn on you that there was something helpful in the message. When you respond to Endogenic longings by being in the Endogenic state, you find greater meaning and resourcefulness in life.

▶ Hunger

A common substitution for Endogenic longing is to confuse psychological hunger with physical hunger. In the Exogenic state, thought replaces sensing and feeling. We can easily learn that eating makes unpleasantness go away, but if the unpleasantness was driven by Endogenic longings, all we did was postpone the needed nurturing. We did not address the longing, but instead ate food when we were actually not hungry. The Endogenic longing will soon return.

Alternatively, when we are in the Endogenic state, we will know if we are thirsty, hungry, or in need of comfort or love. We can distinguish between physical hunger and psychological hunger. It is crucial that we frequently switch to the Endogenic state so we accurately know what we sense and feel. Otherwise, we end up acting without knowing what drives our actions. We end up doing things for the wrong reasons only because we do not switch states. If we need comfort or fulfillment, we must seek it in the Endogenic state.

A simple exercise is to stop the next time you reach for a snack or open the refrigerator. Interrupt the action. Pause, breathe, and switch to the Endogenic state. Sense and feel what is going on inside of yourself in the moment. Are you physically hungry or are you restless, nervous, or uncomfortable? If you do not feel physical hunger, is there some other way you can address your real needs? Do you need comfort, support, or clarity? Are you sensing tension that you have not been able to address, or troubles you have no solution for? These may be triggering Endogenic longings.

You may notice that your urge to eat or drink is often for comfort—like a refuge you yearn for with urgency, in hopes that when you reach it, you can relax. When you are a comfort eater, consider switching to the Endogenic state when you have the impulse to eat. You will instantly know if your urge to eat is out of need for food or due to wanting a refuge. When you stay in the Endogenic state, sensing that you need comfort, it will dawn on you what kind of comfort you need and you can take action accordingly.

▸ Alcohol

Endogenic longings need to be satisfied or they continue to reoccur. When they are satisfied, a sense of relief follows. Those with chronic Exogenic dominance have the most difficulty satisfying Endogenic longings. Sooner or later, most of these individuals discover that alcohol makes a difference.

Alcohol has the effect of temporarily weakening Exogenic dominance. In moderate amounts, it can ease access to the Endogenic state. People who are not familiar with their Endogenic state and who allow alcohol to enable a break from their default state, may feel like a different person as they "let go" in the Endogenic state. Unfortunately, if their Endogenic development has been neglected, what we observe of their Endogenic state is an unrefined raw expression that often surprises themselves and others. Once sober, they feel ashamed and regretful and may rationalize the event as being the fault of the alcohol, as if they take no responsibility for the Endogenic side of themselves.

People who suffer from chronic Exogenic dominance can develop severe problems with alcohol. Endogenic longings may push them to repeat their drinking because they have found no other way of getting close to those longings. They do not know that it takes an active role on their part to find the Endogenic state and protect it. While alcohol can help people temporarily lessen the rigidity of their Exogenic state, it cannot help them build Endogenic reliance.

People who abuse alcohol are pursuing a desperate and destructive substitution for Endogenic fulfillment. Under the influence of alcohol, they are letting go of their own self and their accountability toward others. Overly Exogenic individuals are at risk with alcohol because one can get desperate trying to escape the Exogenic state when Exogenic dominance has taken over an individual's experience of the self.

▸ Addictions

The more society pressures us to be in our Exogenic state, the more dominant our Exogenic state becomes and the less we know how to access our Endogenic state. Dependencies and addictions develop when an individual is incapable of switching to the Endogenic state without the help of a cigarette, a glass of alcohol, or another drug. Drugs are used to escape the Exogenic state—often in response to Endogenic longing. Individuals with an imbalance between Endogenic and Exogenic will be drawn to addictive behavior when they do not know how else to respond to Exogenic dominance.

The plight for highly Exogenic people who cannot switch to the Endogenic state at will is that they try to control their dependency using Exogenic methods. For example, a person who is drawn to drugs or alcohol may limit the use of those substances through willpower and rules. Exchanging one Exogenic behavior for another does not build Endogenic reliance. If a person goes on like this for years, their Endogenic longings will only get stronger and the willpower and rules will have to keep up.

If they instead could strongly rely on their Endogenic state, people would not have to turn to dependencies or addictions. In the Endogenic state, we sense and feel that we are in need, and we can discover how to nurture and fulfill those needs. By learning how to feel safe in the Endogenic state, instead of carrying out an addictive behavior, the individual can connect to sensing and feeling in the Endogenic state.

When a person becomes capable of switching to the Endogenic state every time a temptation occurs, the Exogenic habit can be disrupted. Being in the Endogenic state competes with the external dependency on drugs. Both are not needed. A habit that is not carried out loses its ritual meaning over time and makes the desire for the external substance fade. Individuals can counter their addictions when they have enough Endogenic reliance to learn how to switch from the Exogenic state to the Endogenic state when the addictive desire occurs. Switching to the Endogenic state is empowering to the self, instead of being destructive to the self and others.

Endogenic longings do not need to accumulate and trigger bad consequences. Creating a healthy balance between Endogenic and Exogenic reliance allows us to freely experience both continuously. When the Endogenic state is not dominated, our Endogenic needs can be met. When longings do not build, they do not have to break through a dominant Exogenic state and cause confusion or solicit dependencies. Nurturing and building Endogenic reliance makes every person healthier by supporting a balance between Endogenic and Exogenic.

CHAPTER FORTY-SEVEN

LOVE

*For many people, the newness of Endogenic love eventually gives way to
Exogenic love*

Love always begins with strong and lasting Endogenic moments.
Even a person who rarely experiences Endogenic reliance may
feel strong feelings of love. Only in the Endogenic state can we
feel love that is full of passion, all enveloping, and deeply
fulfilling.

In the Endogenic state, we do not decide what we will sense and
feel, but we notice and receive the signals. With strong Endogenic
reliance, we can be comfortable with the fact that a feeling of
love will come and go. It comes when we connect or relate to
someone or it can come for any reason at all. The feeling goes
away when it is ready to go away, but it may come back again. If
we know to let the Endogenic state unfold and if we know to
access our Endogenic state often, we can experience love over
and over and it will always be new and real. In the Endogenic
state, love is a feeling and sensation that arises in the moment
from within. The Endogenic way of love means we do not try to
control the feeling.

For many people, however, the newness of Endogenic love
eventually gives way to Exogenic love. Because love is such a rich
and fulfilling feeling, anyone who lacks Endogenic reliance will be
afraid that the feeling could go away. The overly Exogenic
individual will unknowingly be seduced to hang on to and control
good Endogenic feelings. Any time you try to control or freeze a
feeling, you are switching to the Exogenic state. In the Exogenic
state, it is possible to hold on to the feeling of love by
remembering and playing out what that feeling was like. Exogenic
love is disconnected from the source that fueled the feeling. It is a
repetition of what was felt before, or a copy of the original.

Most overly Exogenic individuals do not know the difference between feeling the Endogenic feeling of love and hanging on to the memory and idea of that feeling. They just tell themselves that they are in love and that they are committed to have that love never go away. Through discipline and structure, they will repeat the actions, setting, or circumstances that they associate with the memory. It starts unnoticed, but if a person never develops stronger Endogenic reliance, the person will eventually have nothing but Exogenic love, which is very common.

Many people fear, because of what they learn from society, that one day they might wake up and realize they no longer love their partner, or their partner no longer loves them. Whether or not this happens depends very much on whether your love is mostly Endogenic or mostly Exogenic. Those who are capable of Endogenic love know that love is a feeling that occurs in the moment. They remain receptive to feeling and cultivating love. Those who only know Exogenic love will experience love less, and if the Exogenic control is ever dropped, their love is gone.

CHAPTER FORTY-EIGHT

MANIPULATION

*You are powerless to manipulation unless you know how to discern
truth from fiction*

Knowingly and unknowingly, people commonly express the contrary of what they truly think, feel, or want. When you smile at someone you do not like, or agree with someone to avoid conflict, you are overlaying your true thoughts, feelings, or wants with fiction. This form of manipulation has the purpose of achieving an Exogenic goal, for example, to sustain an image about ourselves, preserve a relationship, be liked by others, or avoid conflict. You are powerless to manipulation unless you know how to discern truth from fiction.

When someone communicates to you verbally or non-verbally, through words, action, or inaction, if you happen to be in the Exogenic state, you will probably accept what that person communicated as the truth. In the Exogenic state, we hear words and interpret their meaning without integrating the other data that is available. This is known as accepting something at face value.

If someone shouts at you and says, "I'm not mad," taken at face value, you would believe this statement, but you might notice the inconsistency. In a work environment, however, manipulation is much more hidden. Someone may appear generous or open to your suggestions while they are not at all. They may agree with you but then never act upon it or even act to the contrary. They may ask you questions and state interest because they need you to believe they are interested. They will know from experience that their actions and statements will be believed by almost everyone. This is because almost everyone is in the Exogenic state most of the time in a work environment. People are so used to behaving this way at work that they often are not even aware that they are misleading or manipulating others. It all goes undetected by senders and receivers who are in their Exogenic states.

Anytime you want to counteract manipulation, you can simply switch to your Endogenic state. In your Endogenic state, you can detect mismatches between what you sense and feel and how face value impressions resonate. Sensing someone is mad while that person tells you they are not is an easy application of this. With practice, being in your Endogenic state will give way to an ability to see right through the behaviors of others and confront someone when finding the truth is important.

People who master intentional manipulation of others have developed the skill of keeping both parties in the Exogenic state. You can push someone into the Exogenic state by, for example, speeding up your pace, talking faster, asking questions that require pat answers, behaving superior, or not giving the person a chance to connect to you. Once you get someone in their Exogenic state, your actions and statements will be taken at face value and you can more easily mislead, deceive, or manipulate.

The more time we spend in the Endogenic state, the more we notice the chatter of Exogenic nonsense: people smiling when they are not happy, people nodding their heads in agreement when they do not understand, people chiming in on conversations when they do not know what they are talking about. Anyone with Endogenic strength can discern when communication is Exogenic and devoid of Endogenic substance. In the Endogenic state, we sense and feel the voids and missing links, even as we shift back and forth between the Endogenic and the Exogenic state.

CHAPTER FORTY-NINE

MEASURING CHANGE

Exogenic measurements cannot measure Endogenic change

It is commonly accepted in business that what cannot be measured cannot be managed, and there are many established methods for measuring change in a company. The underlying rationale is to quantify the key drivers of change in order to understand, manage, and improve the performance of the organization. However, it is especially challenging to measure change that results from Endogenic leadership like advances in personal growth, attitude, charisma, presence, willingness, innovation, or strategic drive.

There is an inherent flaw in how most people measure change. As soon as we use Exogenic measurements to measure change, we limit the evaluation to only include Exogenic change. Exogenic measurements cannot measure Endogenic change. Endogenic and Exogenic change must be understood in two different ways.

To improve the leadership capabilities of its managers, a company might start a management development program that includes workshops, retreats, and executive coaching. The person in charge of this program will want to find out if participants became better leaders as a result of participating in the program. The natural tendency is to measure the effectiveness by quantifying how much change occurred.

When you measure change using Exogenic methods, you can accurately measure the Exogenic change that occurred. Clear definitions are critical to measuring Exogenic change. Once top-down goals have been established, Exogenic change can be measured using a mix of subjective measures (such as peer or customer surveys) and objective measures (such as records and logs).

For a management development program, individual mangers can be assessed using pre and post surveys that record feedback from others. You can also measure managers against benchmarks to determine if they are meeting budgets, performing to deadlines, or implementing desired procedures. By comparing data points from before and after the program, change can be measured. Exogenic measurements tell you if a person performs in a certain way. They are meant to compare behaviors and accomplishments to the desired qualities of a leader.

The problem with measuring change occurs when people assume that Exogenic measurements will evaluate Endogenic change. Leadership includes both Endogenic and Exogenic qualities. For example, we may want a leader to become more innovative or develop more charisma, but when Endogenic change is left out of measuring, the results are inaccurate and misleading. This is a problem for forward-looking executives who are making decisions about what works and what does not. When measurements are wrong, conclusions are wrong.

For example, questionnaires with statements and checkboxes are often used to gather input from peers. Those designing the questionnaires probably do not understand Endogenic reliance and their measurements will only reflect Exogenic change. A leader who gains Endogenic reliance is more likely to use time as a resource, but the questionnaire may ask "makes decisions quickly," which ignores this quality. Endogenic reliance makes it easier for a leader to change course or set new directions without being bogged down with inflexibility or fear of change, yet the questionnaire may ask "works consistently toward accomplishing a goal," which measures just the opposite.

Another quality of Endogenic reliance is the ability to anticipate problems. A Duogenic leader, therefore, spends less time putting out fires and more time avoiding crises in the first place. Yet, Exogenic measurements will reward people who are constant firefighters because they appear to be constantly saving the day. Preventing problems from occurring is more valuable for a company, but Exogenic measurements do not pick up on this ability.

People with overly dominant Exogenic states are drawn to rely exclusively on Exogenic measurements because they find reassurance in them. They only see value in making judgments from Exogenic criteria. We can only measure what we have the instruments for. All Exogenic change is measurable because it can be quantified and compared.

The difficulty in assessing Endogenic change, however, is that Endogenic change can only be understood through the senses. Developing Endogenic reliance always involves depths and complexities that can only be discerned. We assess Endogenic change through intensities not definitions, impressions not data points, and discerning not calculating.

One way to understand Endogenic change is through Endogenic self-awareness. In the Endogenic state, your senses are heightened. You may be in a meeting when you discover that in your Endogenic state you easily melded everyone into alignment with just the right statement at just the right time. In the Endogenic state, you can see the moment unfold and you can see the reactions and behaviors of others. You feel at ease and you feel your power as you steer yourself and others exactly where the need lies.

As your Endogenic reliance grows, you feel stronger and more powerful. You may be amazed over what you can do. You may notice that you have a better flow of energy, creativity, inspiration, and wisdom. You may feel agile, free, and flexible. Your self-confidence grows when you experience your capabilities in real time. When the power of the Endogenic state is experienced, you feel inspired and you will choose being in your Endogenic state again when the situation is right. Endogenic self-awareness lets you sense clearly, without a doubt, when your performance has advanced. You will know when you go beyond what you have done before.

Another way to understand Endogenic change is through Endogenic feedback. Sensing Endogenic change in others takes a presence of mind and a state of openness, with no attachment to preconceived notions. By seeking out individuals with strong Endogenic reliance, you can learn from them how your Endogenic qualities are perceived. They may notice the ease with which you accomplish difficult tasks with little resistance, or the ease you have in making accomplishments without complications. They may notice your accuracy in perception and judgment and your capacity to influence others and create synergy instead of compromise. They may be surprised or amazed by the approach you take, the way you think, your ability to see new possibilities, or your charismatic ways with others.

Seeing Endogenic change from the Endogenic state is not linear. Endogenic change is complex and multidimensional. With Endogenic change, the effect or outcome is not only immediate. There is a mid- and long-term element that can easily go unnoticed. With Endogenic change, directions are realigned or transformed over a year or longer.

Endogenic change is best described through narratives. By writing about the thoughts and impressions you gain from Endogenic self-awareness and Endogenic feedback, you can describe your Endogenic qualities, without comparing to a list of expectations. You do not create a quantitative measurement of change. You simply represent what is true at the time.

Feedback from individuals with mostly Exogenic reliance will point at Exogenic strengths and weaknesses. Feedback from individuals with Duogenic reliance will point at Endogenic and Exogenic strengths and weaknesses. With an excess of Exogenic feedback, individuals with Endogenic power are frequently underestimated.

Leaders with strong Endogenic reliance sense their Endogenic strengths. Their self-observations should be part of their company sponsored measurement assessments. A manager, for example, can encourage leaders to submit their own insights gained from Endogenic self-awareness to supplement the Exogenic measurements.

Ultimately, a Duogenic leader draws fully from both Endogenic and Exogenic reliance so that the spontaneity, flexibility, and vision coming from Endogenic reliance are paired with systematic communication and implementation of ideas. A Duogenic leader is able to be agile, strategic, innovative, and spontaneous while also having the skills to plan, organize, compile data, summarize, and replicate.

As a Duogenic leader, you may fare well even with Exogenic measurements, but it will be a struggle to sift through the Exogenic feedback and Exogenic assessments that do not account for your full breadth of capabilities. Some people will criticize you based on assessments that you know are wrong.

The solution for companies that want to advance Duogenic leadership is to ensure that the leaders of organization development understand the limitations of Exogenic measurement and allow Endogenic self-awareness and Endogenic feedback to be an integral component of measuring change and assessing leaders.

CHAPTER FIFTY

MEDITATION

The ultimate benefit of Endogenic meditation is to learn to switch
from Exogenic to Endogenic at will and under any circumstance

Meditation can provide an excellent opportunity for strengthening Endogenic reliance. By focusing on breathing and experiencing the present, we are creating a setting for being in the Endogenic state. However, many people meditate entirely in the Exogenic state. Meditation is possible in the Endogenic state, the Exogenic state, and a combination of both.

If your reason for meditating is self-growth, self-awareness, clarity of mind, inspiration, freedom from stress, or inner peace, these are only achieved while in the Endogenic state and through building Endogenic reliance. By understanding the difference between Endogenic and Exogenic, we can make a more deliberate choice about how we meditate and allow for meditation to be a more fulfilling and valuable practice.

Meditation often begins with a set of rules, for example to stay in a fixed posture, focus on a guided visualization, eliminate thoughts, follow repetitive movements, or recite specific chants. When the rules and structure of meditation force us to concentrate, block out thoughts, or otherwise override our Endogenic state, we are forced to stay in the Exogenic state. Exogenic meditation can help build mental control and increase our willpower to concentrate and direct our thoughts, but it does not build Endogenic strength.

On the other hand, we can use the rules and structure of meditation to set the stage for experiencing our Endogenic state. Finding a quiet place, sitting comfortably, relaxing, and focusing on our breathing all help create a safe environment for being in the Endogenic state. The act of meditating then becomes a time of being in the Endogenic state. This can be an ideal setting for when we seek to rely on our Endogenic state for long periods of time. Endogenic meditation builds Endogenic power.

One common principle in meditation is to eliminate mental distractions, or thoughts. There is a misunderstanding among many practitioners regarding the need to eliminate thought. Thought can occur in the Endogenic state and the Exogenic state. Most people who meditate are intending to experience their Endogenic state, but the act of overriding thoughts places them in the Exogenic state.

Rather than eliminate all thoughts, those seeking Endogenic meditation should only eliminate Exogenic thoughts. To do this, you switch to your Endogenic state. In your Endogenic state, Endogenic thoughts can occur. Endogenic thoughts come unprompted in the form of ideas or sensations that are unrestrained and unique and come and go in their own time frame. For example, you may suddenly become aware of the source of a conflict, even though you did not try to analyze or solve anything.

By meditating in the Endogenic state, we can allow our Endogenic thoughts to occur in the moment. When that happens, we conceive something new about ourselves and expand our Endogenic self-awareness. When we have an Endogenic thought, as soon as we dwell on that thought or try to stop having that thought, we have switched to the Exogenic state. To find our way back to the Endogenic state, we allow thoughts to come and go without controlling our thinking.

We move from the Endogenic state to the Exogenic instantly. Being in the Endogenic state for long and at will can be extremely challenging because we switch easily and unknowingly to the Exogenic state. Meditation helps us set aside time to notice which state we are in and to choose to experience our Endogenic state in a safe setting. Endogenic power comes from being in the Endogenic state and from knowing how to switch between Endogenic and Exogenic. The ultimate benefit of Endogenic meditation is to learn to switch from Exogenic to Endogenic at will and under any circumstance.

CHAPTER FIFTY-ONE

MOTIVATION

*Endogenic motivation is like a hunger where we latch onto a pursuit
because it feels like it is meant for us*

When you are motivated, it is because either you have a goal in mind or you have a sense of passion, or both. Motivation is a driving force that leads to success and fulfillment, and most people want more motivation in life. To increase motivation for yourself and others, you need to either identify appealing goals or find what makes you curious. Being motivated by an achievement or goal is Exogenic motivation and being motivated from curiosity, passion, or having fun is Endogenic motivation.

With Exogenic motivation, it takes discipline and commitment to reach the goal. By identifying a realistic structure, process, plan, or steps, we work to achieve the goal. We make goals happen by sticking to commitments. Empowerment follows as we find ourselves on the right path of filling the gap between where we are and where we want to be.

In contrast, Endogenic motivation is like a hunger where we latch onto a pursuit because it feels like it is meant for us. A deep satisfaction comes from the sense that what we do is personally relevant and meaningful. Endogenic motivation does not follow a prescribed path or goal. It unfolds on its own, and as the individual makes discoveries and decides what to do with them, goals may be part of the outcome.

Most high points in life are gained through a combination of Endogenic and Exogenic motivation. For example, learning to write is a chore for every child, but many start loving it and may even become gifted writers. Or the repetitive learning of a musical instrument may unfold a brilliance otherwise untapped. In business, the greatest leaps in innovation occur when motivation begins from Endogenic passion and curiosity. Implementing those discoveries, or taking an idea from prototype to production, requires Exogenic discipline and structure.

A model for successful innovation in business is to create an environment that allows and encourages Endogenic motivation to coexist with Exogenic limitations and realities. Most business leaders, even though they want innovation, unknowingly kill Endogenic motivation by imposing Exogenic goals too soon or by overpowering Endogenic reliance with Exogenic demands like definitions, parameters, rules, and processes.

CHAPTER FIFTY-TWO

PATIENCE

In the Endogenic state, patience does not start with discipline; it starts with noticing one's frustration

When it seems like your team is not working hard enough, does not adapt fast enough, is not staying enough on task, or does not communicate its needs well enough, frustration builds. What should a leader do when capable, competent, and usually successful team members are not meeting expectations? The temptation is to push harder, be more critical, or express disappointment. However, you may have learned from experience that when you come down hard and show your frustration, it only creates resentment, becomes counterproductive, and demotivates employees.

Managers who have already pushed their employees hard, often end up concluding that they should not act on their frustration and instead be more patient because they do not want to be micromanagers. They commit to more patience, but still nothing really changes. One day in a meeting, their accumulated restrained frustration might break through and they could find themselves pushing in the same ineffective way again. Having more patience becomes impossible to implement and the cycle begins again: push hard, have patience, problem not solved, push harder.

To assume that patience is missing is due to confusion between Endogenic and Exogenic reliance. The Exogenic approach to being patient is implemented by being passive, not criticizing, and waiting. We refrain ourselves from expressing our frustration, which takes discipline and the ability to contain ourselves. If pushing hard causes organizational withdrawal, then easing up is thought to be the answer.

But neither easing up or showing more frustration is constructive when a team does not meet expectations despite the priority and urgency being clear. Both approaches only waste more time.

Patience can alternatively be approached by switching to the Endogenic state. Being in the Endogenic state lets us discover missing links, voids, and gaps that limit accountability and expediency. In the Endogenic state, patience does not start with discipline; it starts with noticing one's frustration. When one is frustrated in the Endogenic state, one will know what the frustration is about. One will understand what needs to be expressed. One can uncover the source of the frustration rather than blow up, blame others, withdraw, or take over.

With Endogenic patience, you enable yourself to have space for empathy, listening, exploring, understanding, inspiring, and participating. Practically, this means making yourself available to listen and understand, interacting with those who are working on the challenge, being approachable, and checking in with people to see where they can, with a little facilitation, untie a knot or visualize new strategic paths.

We nurture Endogenic patience by engaging with people, immersing ourselves in the problem with them, experiencing its multiple facets, and seeking solutions with those involved. For example, if deadlines are slipping, experiencing this through their eyes, and feeling the frustration, may lead you to enable new plans or access new resources that resolve the situation. When much is at stake and urgency matters, it is more productive to engage and clarify the path with all involved than to insert fear, add pressure, place blame, or wait passively.

CHAPTER FIFTY-THREE

PERCEPTION

The more uncertainty you have capacity for, the more you will learn from your perception

Perceiving is the act of seeing, hearing, or becoming aware of something through the senses. It is the basis of all learning. When we are in the Endogenic state, perception is our rich, unfiltered, unique awareness of what we see, think, feel, sense, or experience.

For Endogenic learning, it is important that perception be treasured and pondered and not quickly categorized or discarded. As soon as you start to do something with your perception, you have switched to your Exogenic state. This is not bad, because ultimately we need to reach conclusions and assess where we stand, but the more balance you have between Endogenic learning and Exogenic learning and the more uncertainty you have capacity for, the more you will learn from your perception. It is our over-reliance on the Exogenic state that limits what we can perceive.

Unless you have a strong Endogenic state, you apply and direct most of your perceptions without realizing it. Exogenic learning is a constant application of perception as opposed to a constant experiencing of perception. By being in the Endogenic state more frequently and experiencing perception, you develop a greater capacity for uncertainty and can start to reverse the long-term damage caused by overly Exogenic learning.

By knowing if you are in your Endogenic or Exogenic state, you can begin to recognize the moments when you stop learning from perception. These are moments of opportunity when you can choose to benefit from your perception or not.

Three major barriers limit our ability to experience perception and force us to switch from Endogenic to Exogenic reliance:

▸ 1. Replace Your Perceptions with Beliefs

A quick way to reject an Endogenic perception is to fall back on your beliefs. By replacing perception with belief, your conflict is gone, but you forfeit the possibility of learning something new. You continue to believe what you already know.

In the Exogenic state, instead of embracing our unique perceptions, we overpower them with what we already accept as beliefs and opinions. We mistake beliefs and opinions for truth, and we feel safe with them. This leads us to dismiss new findings easily.

For example, a coworker might suggest using a certain marketing service to communicate with customers about a product update. You might be quick to point out that you know of a better service that is inexpensive and easy to use. You know this because you used the service once or read about it recently. We constantly reject ideas, dismiss thoughts, and make conclusions based on our beliefs and opinions. The moment your preexisting opinion about marketing services kicked in, you were done learning. It did not occur to you to explore the presented idea, ask questions, or ponder the thought. You missed out by not learning about the other service your coworker was familiar with, which might have better delivery rates or offer a more professional looking campaign.

As soon as a situation appears similar to what we know or have heard of, we tend to trust our beliefs instead of retrieving further data from perception and diversifying our knowledge. We then simply respond to what we already know and stop perceiving.

A vulnerability of being in the Exogenic state is that it eliminates the distinction between perceptions and beliefs. By confusing perceptions with beliefs, we create limitations in life.

If you become comfortable with Endogenic learning, you can begin to overcome this barrier by noticing the moments when you stop perceiving. It is possible to notice the very moment when you disregard perception. At that moment, ask yourself, "Do I still perceive? Could I perceive more?" When you increase your Endogenic power, you can afford to have fewer beliefs. As you begin to favor perception over beliefs, you can more easily question your beliefs and seek to perceive more. You will accept other points of view, be curious about them, and have insights to share with others.

▸ 2. Confirm Your Perception is Universal

Another barrier to Endogenic perception is our eagerness to seek confirmation from others. With low Endogenic reliance, you will find it difficult to trust your perception when it is not confirmed by others. For example, if you have doubts about a speaker at a conference you might ask some of your colleagues about their impressions. If they all are in awe about the speaker, and if you lack Endogenic confidence, you will likely dismiss your perception and accept the consensus of the group.

We seek confirmation to prove that our perception is universal. This could be a simple whisper to the person next to you like, "Did you see that?" By finding confirmation of your perception, you take that confirmation as assurance that your perception reflects a truth beyond your subjective world. You gain certainty about what you perceive when you believe it is shared.

When we confirm our perception, we switch to the Exogenic state and categorize the perception as being valid. If one person does not confirm our perception, we can try another. We tend to seek confirmation from like-minded people because it provides a greater success rate.

You can choose to reduce your need for confirmation and increase your accuracy of perception instead. By noticing the very moment in which you would seek confirmation, you have the opportunity to ponder the perception instead. When you ponder a perception, you learn from the perception. This is Endogenic learning.

If you are too quick to seek confirmation, you limit your intelligence. Not only do you perceive less, but because you do not often seek confirmation from those who would differ from your perception, your beliefs and opinions become narrower over time.

▸ 3. Reject Your Perception

What if you noticed tremendous potential in a coworker who others only joke about and label as "odd" or "difficult?" You may not understand why you feel this, but the perception is clear. When you hint about this person's potential to coworkers, you get a negative reaction. Everyone you trust seems to write the person off. You feel alone to have such a perception and begin to question your perception. If you are like most people, you soon find yourself rejecting your perception and agreeing with the others.

If we have perceptions that are embarrassing, bizarre, destructive, or go against the beliefs of the majority, others around us are not going to confirm those perceptions. We will think we are the only one who perceives that way. Most people habitually and quickly reject a unique perception rather than explore it in the Endogenic state.

If you are mostly an Exogenic learner, you commonly reject perceptions that do not hold up to Exogenic standards. Exogenic learning teaches us to seek permanent truth, rules, and standards, and to fit in with others around us. However, when you also accept Endogenic learning, you come to know that you are alone with many of your perceptions. They are your perceptions, and they are unique. If you become comfortable with this idea and comfortable with uncertainty, you will not be so driven to seek confirmation or rejection of your perceptions. You will let your perceptions have a life of their own, and you will welcome perceptions even if they seem strange or unexpected.

Endogenic learners often discover that a unique perception, such as the unexplained feeling that a coworker has great potential, later turns out to be fully founded and insightful. Welcoming your perception, questioning it, and exploring it may lead to keener observation. You may go on to discover that there are reasons for your perception. Being open to observation may lead you to discover that you were right. Others around you who reject their unique perceptions are operating with reduced awareness.

When others say they know the truth, we do not question if that is based on Endogenic perception or Exogenic belief. As a result, even though other people have similar perceptions as you, you may never find out because they voice their beliefs instead of their perceptions. They are telling you what they believe they are supposed to think, feel, or do. When you have a personal or work relationship with a highly Exogenic person, you may feel like you cannot really know this person or you cannot find a depth to their personality or you always seem to get pat answers to what should be provocative questions.

CHAPTER FIFTY-FOUR

POSITIONAL POWER

A leader who is in the Endogenic state knows whether admiration
comes from the Endogenic or Exogenic state

When a person acquires status, title, rank, wealth, or another form of Exogenic positional power, they often lose touch with their Endogenic confidence. With positional power, you will be treated with more respect by almost everyone who knows your rank.

Positional power always comes with the ability to grant power or privileges to others. Those who might benefit from your resources seek to be in good agreement with you.

Most people with positional power forget that they are being treated the way they are because their resources are appreciated. When special treatment becomes a daily occurrence, they assume it is because of who they are, not how they rank. The treatment they receive is Exogenic, and it is purposed for a goal.

A leader who is in the Endogenic state, however, knows whether admiration comes from the Endogenic or Exogenic state. Endogenic respect is sincerely appreciated because, like all people, leaders prefer to be respected for who they are at the core, not for their title or position.

Many leaders who have retired from high-level positions in large corporations are puzzled by how quickly they are forgotten by the industry and their former coworkers. Stripped of their positional power, they soon miss the Exogenic confidence that had been fueled by the daily respect and attention they used to receive due to their position.

A dominant Exogenic leader may feel resentful over this loss and become cynical or behave entitled, whereas a Duogenic leader can adjust to change more easily and continue to build Endogenic power.

CHAPTER FIFTY-FIVE

POSITIVE THINKING

Positive thinking builds a reality that fits our comfort level, instead of challenging our comfort level to keep up with reality

In the Endogenic state, we often feel vulnerable or uncertain. A simple way to get rid of those feelings is to switch to the Exogenic state by hanging on to a thought. When we make ourselves believe a thought, it can replace our feelings of vulnerability, and uncertainty goes away. An application of this tool is known as "positive thinking." The guidance is to override a negative feeling or thought with a positive thought. We have a desire to make ourselves safe and comfortable, but it becomes counterproductive when the negative feeling or thought was accurate and the positive thought is make-believe.

To make sure we do not cause a new problem, we must distinguish between Endogenic and Exogenic. Positive thinking is never a problem when we override an Exogenic thought with another Exogenic thought. But overriding an Endogenic feeling or thought with an Exogenic thought compromises the truth.

For example, if someone was considered for a promotion and was rejected due to budget constraints, rather than accepting the hurt over the disappointment, the person might just want to completely forget about it and behave positive, as if nothing had happened. This Exogenic override prevents the individual from sensing and feeling and comprehending the frustration. Such pain can come back as self-doubt and cause irrational distrust in one's own leadership strength, without knowing why.

When we suppress strong sensations, they likely come back in a more hidden and perhaps twisted form. By relying only on the Exogenic state, through positive thinking, Endogenic pain becomes inaccessible and abstract. Overriding the Endogenic state can corrupt our judgment when we no longer have direct access to what fueled the pain.

Fear of the Endogenic state makes the Exogenic state more dominant. What we lose is feeling and sensing the present and being in touch with what comes from within. We reduce familiarity with the power that lies within and instead focus on the power we have to change things with discipline and recipes. With that, we create a new balance where instead of relying on the state that is most appropriate for the situation, we rely on the Exogenic state—the state we are most comfortable with. In the Exogenic state, we dictate to ourselves what we think, do, and feel. Positive thinking builds a reality that fits our comfort level, instead of challenging our comfort level to keep up with reality.

CHAPTER FIFTY-SIX

POWER ABUSE

Individuals who lack Endogenic reliance are confused about power,
which is true for a majority of leaders

People who chronically overpower their Endogenic state with Exogenic dominance are prone to abuse power—be it a manager who bosses others around, a teacher who rejects nonstandard work, a parent who emotionally rejects a child, or a sales clerk who misleads a customer.

Endogenic reliance nurtures the soul, which creates a deep sense of security. But if you lack Endogenic reliance, it is likely you will instead seek security through Exogenic achievements, importance, control, and power.

We gain Exogenic security when we think about or are reminded by others of how important we are, what we have accomplished, goals we pursue, how well we fit in, and how we stand out in the eyes of others. These reminders counter thoughts of insecurity, helplessness, inferiority, and forlornness. That is why it matters that we have awards, trophies, titles, social affiliations, influential friends, or other reminders of our importance displayed for others to see. Exogenic security is manifested through having followers, affirmers, and admirers.

When we are not reminded of the security, it seems missing. This creates an endless need for acceptance, praise, or sense of superiority. The result is that people who chronically overpower their Endogenic state with Exogenic dominance use power over others to generate enough reminders to feel secure. The more powerfully positioned in society they are, the greater the chance they will misuse that power.

Using positional power to make yourself feel secure is an egocentric use of power. Individuals who have not developed a base of Endogenic personal power tend to over-rely on positional power and do not easily give up the control they wield with their Exogenic authority. They will seek to secure their power by making their position clear to everyone and they wrongly assume that people respect them for who they are instead of the position they hold. Individuals who lack Endogenic reliance are confused about power, which is true for a majority of leaders in business and social settings.

Endogenic reliance is the source of good situational judgment. Without that, leaders tie their judgment to the norms of their environment. When their environment is filled with borderline moral or ethical conduct and that conduct is perceived as the norm, those lacking Endogenic reliance do not sense that anything is wrong.

Exogenic judgment goes by what is permitted, not what feels right, and small deviations from the norm seem trivial. That is why a power abusing parent can threaten a child knowing that many parents do the same, or a manager can intimidate employees knowing that the sales goals need to be met, or a teacher can demoralize a student knowing that students are supposed to respect them anyway, or a CEO can demand huge personal sacrifices from the management team knowing they will comply out of fear of losing their jobs.

Everything is different for the individual who can develop Endogenic reliance and balance that with their Exogenic positional power. In the Endogenic state, judgment is gauged by what we sense and how it feels. When it does not feel right, it is not right. If we would not want something for ourselves, we do not want to force it on others, even when everyone else says or thinks otherwise.

Even if we have accepted a certain norm for decades, with Endogenic strength we may someday reject it. People with Endogenic strength are the people who dare to do what they feel is right. They pioneer business environments that cultivate mutual respect, invent new concepts in education, and inspire more compassion and understanding in the lives of others. In the Endogenic state, we find fulfillment in actions that feel right.

Becoming part of a hierarchically established structure creates a conflict between adapting to perceived norms and independence in decision-making. The more Endogenic confidence a person has, the less the person has a need to adapt to the environment. A leader with Endogenic confidence has more independence, is less concerned with fulfilling other's expectations, and is less susceptible to compromising on values. With Endogenic strength, you have no desire to detach from your own values or fit into an environment. Instead, you are able to lead the environment. The more connected you feel with the environment you influence, the more accountable you feel for your choices. Leaders with Endogenic power feel responsible for wrongdoings related to integrity, morals, and ethics and are therefore less susceptible to abusing their power.

CHAPTER FIFTY-SEVEN

RATIONALIZING

*If we do not recognize rationalizations, we may misinterpret them as a
sign of strength*

Rationalizations are explanations and justifications used to cover-up Endogenic feelings, thoughts, or actions that we want to reject or hide from others. Lack of Endogenic reliance makes us want to disregard Endogenic feelings, thoughts, or actions that surface. We do not understand them and hope we can repair the damage they may have caused by convincing ourselves and others that those Endogenic parts do not exist.

We hear rationalizations every day. They range from detailed excuses about why a person does not want to take a risk to small cover-ups meant to undo verbal slipups. If we do not recognize rationalizations, we may misinterpret them as a sign of strength. However, rationalizations signal that a person is out of balance and lacks Endogenic reliance.

Rationalizations are a prominent challenge at work and are hard to penetrate. For example, many talented and innovative leaders are hesitant to talk openly to high-ranking overly Exogenic managers with more positional power. They fear their work will be criticized or they will be unable to convince others of its merit. Rather than admit to themselves or to others that they are afraid to engage top executives and address their concerns, they will rationalize avoiding such a meeting. They may explain that their project is not quite far enough along to support their point or that they can succeed without top stakeholder buy-in or that the top executive will not have an open ear anyway. The rationalization will make complete sense to them and others, and it will demonstrate that the person is in control. The effect, however, is that rationalizations build walls, limit progress, and reduce a person's influence.

When we meet a person who has a strong fear of the Endogenic state, that person will usually appear to be in complete control. But we might have a sense that we do not always trust this person. Sometimes we may notice a behavior that is atypical, like an unexpected sharp verbal jab or a seemingly harmless joke with a mean or inappropriate undertone. We may wonder if that atypical side will come back. If the person realizes that they made a slipup, they will try to explain what happened. We will hear rationalizations, such as "I was just kidding" or "I wasn't thinking" or "I was in a bad mood" or "You shouldn't be so sensitive." It really means that they are trying to keep up their Exogenic mask of being in complete control but accidentally let their guard down.

When we find ourselves making detailed excuses or justifying slipups, the right reaction is to have insightful acceptance and to learn from the event. This is a way that we can embrace our Endogenic state instead of succumbing to fear. A rationalization should trigger thoughts about why we reacted in that manner. Our Endogenic thoughts and actions are often full of great meaning, and noticing them can provide access to truths that make us stronger.

CHAPTER FIFTY-EIGHT

REBELLION

Regardless of whether we call it the terrible twos, teenage rebellion, or midlife crisis, Endogenic rebellion can occur at any time in life

Endogenic rebellion is the healthy act of unknowingly rejecting violence against the self caused by Exogenic dominance. The purpose is to rebalance our reliance between Endogenic and Exogenic. Regardless of whether we call it the terrible twos, teenage rebellion, or midlife crisis, Endogenic rebellion can occur at any time in life. The disruption, confusion, and emotional turmoil that can occur when we protect our Endogenic state should not be feared and avoided, but rather welcomed as a path to personal growth and strength.

The Endogenic state dominates during early childhood. Ideally, as children grow, they develop Endogenic and Exogenic strength equally. Endogenic reliance develops naturally as young children spend hours being inquisitive, creating fantasies, questioning everything, and touching, tasting, and sensing the world. They also naturally develop Exogenic reliance through imitating others, role-playing, repetition, building motor skills, learning rules, understanding limits, comparing themselves to others, categorizing, and exploring ways to fit in.

What we classify as the Terrible Twos in young children is an Endogenic state rebellion. It is a protest by children to ensure that the environment does not forcibly override their Endogenic state. Children naturally protect being in the Endogenic state. The Endogenic state is the purest sense of being alive, and young children have not yet learned the value of Exogenic rules, customs, plans, discipline, or delayed gratification.

As parents start the teaching process of self-protection and conformity, children discover they are not allowed to go where they want, touch what they want, taste what they want, or sleep when they want. They are repeatedly told "no" for their own safety. They must learn rules and accept authority as they are told to wear clothes, eat with utensils, be quiet, sit still, or be strapped into a car seat. The rules and guidelines parents learn and the concerns they have for the well-being of their children are imposed on the children.

From the child's perspective, these controls and limitations are sometimes forcibly imposed upon them from outside. This is their early taste of Exogenic dominance, and all children reject that dominance to some degree. Young children's Endogenic states are strong, so they freely voice their objections. The harder the parents push Exogenic dominance, the more dramatically the child fights back. The child is caught in an impossible situation. Without adequate words, the child communicates through crying, screaming, kicking, and running.

This is the time when unaware parents focus too much on making sure their child obeys, is well mannered, and fits the model of a perfect child. If the child's Endogenic state is not respected, the parents risk harming their child's Endogenic spirit. The parents either fight back harder with increasing forcefulness or they start to learn from their child that overpowering and control is a form of violence. The more aware the parents are of their own Endogenic strength, the more they see their child's predicament and can help the child grow both Endogenic and Exogenic strength in union.

What we call teenage rebellion is another common attempt at Endogenic state rebellion. It is a protest by the young adult to ensure that the environment does not permanently override or destroy their Endogenic reliance. For most teens, the ratio between Endogenic and Exogenic strength has developed in favor of the Exogenic state, leaving the Endogenic state underutilized and easily overpowered.

Adolescence provides an opportunity to rebalance the ratio between Endogenic and Exogenic reliance. Young adults reach an age where they find they have more influence over their own thoughts and actions than ever before. This opens new possibilities for them to experience the spontaneity, creativity, curiosity, and passion of their Endogenic state and allows them to experience life in a unique new way.

What the teen sees as a desire to conquer the world, discover new meaning, and find new identity is interpreted by overly Exogenic adults as pushing the boundaries, breaking the rules, and rejecting what is already established. The teen may not feel any rebellion at all, but the Exogenic environment labels it as such.

As society fights against teenage rebellion through stricter rules and controls, most teens feel that something has been taken from them or that society is ignorant of what is important. To benefit from this conflict, it is important for young adults to develop their Endogenic reliance and learn that they do not need to seek only conformity. Unfortunately, few individuals at that age have a strong Endogenic state because they have already been deprived from developing it fully. If they cannot find Endogenic strength, they merely swap one sort of Exogenic reliance, (parental rules and parental support) for another sort of Exogenic reliance (peer group rules and peer group support).

As we get older, more and more effort goes into obtaining goals and status. The societal norm is that the Exogenic state dominates over the Endogenic state. For most people, the degree and frequency of overpowering the Endogenic state increases with age. We continue building an imbalance of Exogenic dominance.

A midlife crisis is yet another Endogenic state rebellion. Just like the terrible twos or teenage rebellion, we are unknowingly attempting to protect our Endogenic state from chronic domination. Exogenic strength does not make up for a lack of Endogenic strength. If we have an imbalance, it accumulates over time and leads to a crisis. Midlife does not create a crisis—the crisis occurs when we struggle to regain balance between Endogenic and Exogenic reliance.

We may think a midlife crisis is normal because everybody appears to have one. Although we may call this a crisis, it is actually a healthy opportunity for establishing better psychological balance. As we question our identity and the meaning we have accepted for our life, we begin to rebel against our customs, habits, and status quo. It is an attempt to disrupt the trajectory we have set for our life.

There are two ways people deal with their midlife crisis. One is to rely even more on Exogenic answers like a new car, new house, improved image, more status, or rationalizing that things are not so bad. The other is to spend much more time in the Endogenic state through self-awareness, contemplation, and making space for freedom, relaxation, and immersing in the moment. The first way leads to becoming even more unbalanced and unsatisfied and the second leads to becoming more authentic and fulfilled.

When a crisis is not addressed correctly, we tend to think that we did what we could. We rationalize that the quality of life dissipates with age. We think that it is normal to have big hopes and not see them fulfilled, or we believe that losing enthusiasm means being realistic, and we keep setting expectations lower so they better match our experience of life. We pass this learning on to the next generation to help prevent their disappointments.

A myth about aging is that we assume the sense of wholeness and confidence we once had was a product of youth, while in fact it was a product of Endogenic and Exogenic balance. We see younger people and envy their fresh hopes and aspirations. We feel nostalgic about what we have lost, and take comfort out of calling it a midlife crisis. While it may seem normal for a person to conclude that life is incremental and repetitive, it is only that way when we are in the Exogenic state.

When people fail in their Endogenic rebellion, they continue to increase Exogenic dominance. Their personality becomes more rigid, self-righteous, controlling, and set in its ways. By missing the opportunity to develop new Endogenic power, the individual further develops a false persona and becomes less creative, less comfortable adapting to new environments, bitter toward youth, and condescending toward the Endogenic state in themselves and others.

The need for restoring Endogenic strength is intuitively felt by people who make statements like, "I want to smell the roses," or "I need to do what I love." They are sensing their Endogenic longing.

The best outcome of an Endogenic rebellion is for the individual to embrace the Endogenic state and begin to build more reliance that is Endogenic. A successful Endogenic rebellion results in the individual gaining a better balance between the Endogenic state and the Exogenic state. With that comes a newfound power of resourcefulness, openness, and curiosity toward life.

Endogenic rebellion carries the potential for a surge in personal growth, unfolding new Endogenic strength and rekindling Endogenic abilities like creativity, intuition, clarity, vision, passion, influence, fulfillment, spontaneity, empathy, and authenticity. With less Exogenic overpowering, an individual has less desire for control and rigidity, and greater influence over choosing between the Endogenic and Exogenic state as situations demand.

CHAPTER FIFTY-NINE

REJECTED THOUGHTS AND FEELINGS

With strong Exogenic reliance and weak Endogenic reliance, we are constantly tempted to reject thoughts and feelings that are incompatible with what we want

We do not choose our Endogenic thoughts and feelings. They happen on their own as a manifestation of being in the Endogenic state. Many of us assume that by not thinking certain thoughts, those thoughts will not exist, but this is only true if we switch to the Exogenic state where we can prevent thoughts that could come from sensing and feeling. The Exogenic state eliminates the requirement for sensing and feeling. Instead, it builds on a conceivable thought and generates emotion and behavior accordingly.

Sometimes our Endogenic thoughts or feelings alarm us. We might be shocked to notice that we were thinking about harming someone or that we feel hatred toward someone we think we should like. With strong Exogenic reliance and weak Endogenic reliance, we are constantly tempted to reject thoughts and feelings that are incompatible with what we want. This is self-limiting. Rather than control a feeling or thought, we need to control whether or not we will act upon a feeling or thought. For that, we need to know what we sense and feel. Controlling actions, such as what we say or do, is the healthy Exogenic function of self-control. Endogenic thoughts should be acknowledged, and the Exogenic state should be used to not act on a feeling when a corresponding action ought not to occur.

The greater our fear of the Endogenic state, the more we attempt to control our feelings and thoughts when things become vague or ambivalent. Instead of pondering, we just reject or deny. We can make Endogenic thoughts and feelings go away with Exogenic thought. For example, we may feel angry but decide to feel unfazed instead. We just tell ourselves that we are not angry and reject the feeling of anger. Others may see that we appear even-tempered, but their impression is the result of our Exogenic control. As long as we stay in control, we will be able to feel the way we think we feel. However, the Endogenic feeling may be back anytime. It can surface at a moment we are not prepared for. It may sneak into one of our actions or our tone of voice. If someone comments on that, we will be surprised or insulted because we will have forgotten that the feeling existed.

If you unexpectedly blow up at your colleague, you may be surprised that you let that happen. The source of that blow up might have originated days or weeks earlier. Perhaps you resented something your coworker did or believed but you rejected your negative reaction because you did not want to feel resentment. Over time, you tried to forget what you knew and forget that you resented it. Then you blow up. Often, when people blow up, they remember the sting that had fueled the resentment. Therefore, they mistakenly blame themselves for remembering the hurt. They think if they could forget what they resent, they would not blow up. They conclude that if they do not have the negative memory, they will not have to resent the person.

The best way to prevent a feeling or thought from becoming an unwanted action is to turn to the Endogenic state. When we have a strong feeling or thought and it reoccurs, we need to take care of it by exploring it in the Endogenic state. Exploring thoughts and feelings in the Endogenic state will allow them to transform on their own. For example, resentment can change to mourning over a lost hope and from there to acceptance and eventually compassion.

When we are in the Endogenic state, we can become aware of what we think, what we sense, what we feel, and what we do. But when we are in the Exogenic state, we do not know what we sense and feel. We only know what we think we feel or what we want to feel. We have no choice but to act without knowing what feelings we act from. We may be surprised about our actions.

Suppressed feelings slip out unexpectedly. Only after we slip up can we find out what we really were feeling.

Individuals with a strong fear of the Endogenic state are used to being negatively surprised by themselves. They have come to assume that not thinking certain thoughts will not manifest those thoughts. Then the assumption proves itself wrong, and the person concludes that inappropriate behavior lies dormant within. Such a person relies on control to suppress it and builds Exogenic instead of Endogenic reliance.

The more a person relies on the Exogenic state to control the Endogenic state, the greater the tendency for unwanted and unexpected thought and behavior. This aggravates the lack of feeling safe in oneself and builds greater Exogenic and lesser Endogenic reliance. It is a common cycle among people with dominant Exogenic states.

CHAPTER SIXTY

RESILIENCE

*If our Endogenic reliance is weak, a crisis can easily turn into a deep
identity crisis*

The strength and balance of our Endogenic and Exogenic states has an enormous impact on our lives when a crisis occurs. For example, a loved one dies, we lose our job, we have a serious illness, or we are accused of wrongdoing. When the environment changes drastically, the flood of feelings and thoughts is too much for the Exogenic state to define and regulate. The impact of the threat overwhelms our walls of control and order that we had put in place with Exogenic reliance. Complexities and complications make Exogenic reliance reach a breaking point and collapse.

In an extreme crisis, an individual may feel as though they lost everything. Endogenic reliance becomes pivotal. Regardless of the quantifiable hardship, the weaker the Endogenic state, the more acute a crisis becomes. When Exogenic reliance collapses, we have no choice but to switch to the Endogenic state and feel the fear. The less familiar we are with our Endogenic state, the more dangerous such a crisis will appear.

If our Endogenic reliance is weak, a crisis can easily turn into a deep identity crisis. Most people first try to solve their identity crisis the wrong way. They look to the Exogenic state. They learn from others that they should just try harder, do better, forget the bad stuff, snap out of it, and stop thinking of "poor me." The advice is wrong. A crisis can only be resolved through turning to Endogenic reliance. It starts with listening well to your self, doing more of what you want instead of what you think you should want, and by rediscovering how to feel safe while in the Endogenic state. In the Endogenic state, you find strength by being in the present moment.

For individuals with very weak Endogenic reliance, it does not take a tragedy to cause a breakdown. With over-reliance on the Exogenic state, many illusions take hold in a person's life, like being the smartest, best-looking, toughest, or most deserving person. Any illusion we place great value on, when it collapses, can result in a significant breakdown.

Whatever the cause of a breakdown, there is a gain to letting go. When you hit bottom and feel things cannot get worse, you stop holding onto what you already lost. You start accepting what you experience. You allow yourself to experience the Endogenic state, and you begin to find Endogenic strength. It is only in the Endogenic state that you can truly overcome your fear of the Endogenic state. In the midst of overbearing fear, you realize that being in the Endogenic state is not dangerous. The better you can face your fear while in the Endogenic state and let go of trying to control, the more effective you are at navigating a crisis and finding new paths to recover. Noticing your fears carries the opportunity to build Endogenic power.

CHAPTER SIXTY-ONE

RISK TAKING

*With Endogenic confidence, what appears to others as risky is actually
an obvious next step that does not feel risky at all*

Taking on too much risk or avoiding risks altogether are both
symptoms of low Endogenic confidence.

Endogenic confidence gives a person the ability to gauge how
much risk to take on. Managing risk requires knowing how to
tune in and take the pulse of a situation. With Endogenic
confidence, what appears to others as risky is actually an obvious
next step that does not feel risky at all.

With strong Endogenic confidence, you can have clarity about
complex situations. You simply know what to do. Observers
admire this and call it courage. They think you took a big risk
because they do not know about all the Endogenic strength that
was behind your decision. Duogenic strength allows a leader to
draw upon an entire lifetime of experience, combined with clarity
in the moment, to make a decision without the burden of
carefully itemizing all the thousands of data points, weighing and
ranking the pros and cons, and worrying about failure.

On the other hand, without Endogenic confidence, people will
move forward banking on hit or miss. Risky decisions are made
by carefully assessing a traceable line of facts and figures, and
then going with where the data takes them. They believe risk
taking is part of the job, like jumping off a cliff now and then. If
they succeed, they will believe it was due to their superior
methodology, but in part it was due to luck, because when dealing
with unknown complexities, no amount of facts and figures can
ever be enough. If they fail, they will believe it was due to faulty
information, and it will be easy to find blame. Observers who do
not know the difference between Endogenic and Exogenic see

the lucky hit and admire the person for taking such a risk, but taking big risks without Endogenic confidence is haphazard, accident prone, or even irresponsible.

CHAPTER SIXTY-TWO

SELF-MENTORING

You have the ability to drastically change the nature of any moment by simply asking one question

Every second, the consequences of your action or inaction will change the course of your future. This is true even if you pay no attention. You have the ability to drastically change the nature of any moment by simply asking one question. This question is like a fork in the road. You can turn or not. You can notice it or not. Simply ask yourself "What state am I in right now?"

Every time you ask yourself what state you are in, you become an advisor or mentor to yourself. What you do with your answer is your chance to invent your life in that moment. Every moment contains everything available for shaping the future. You build your personal life through your use of the moment at hand. Only if you know what state you are in can you know if you want to switch to the other.

There is always a choice about which state you are in. When you choose between your Endogenic and Exogenic states, you access the power of either state, not just the one you usually rely on. The power of both states lies within you. Sometimes your default state is wrong for the moment. Sometimes, switching to the other state creates a new opportunity, offers new potential, or helps you bring a task to closure. Any time, and under any circumstance, you can instantly access, increase, or direct your energy and strength. You can intensify your power and show it if you want.

The more frequently you ask yourself, the more often you will choose the best state for the moment. Being a mentor to yourself provides you with opportunities that other people cannot provide for you. Through repeated awareness of knowing what state you are in and through your action of choice, you will grow yourself into the person you wish to be.

CHAPTER SIXTY-THREE

SELF-RESPECT

*The only way to build self-respect is to increase your Endogenic
reliance. It is a personal discovery of who you are*

Confidence looks powerful. When we see a highly confident person, we may think, "If I could be like that, then I would respect myself more." Most people try to build self-respect as an Exogenic quest. However, such a quest leads to stress, burnout, or depression, without achieving the desired results.

Once an overly Exogenic person recognizes that trying hard is a constant struggle without gain, that person becomes trapped. In the Exogenic state, it seems like the only alternative to trying harder is doing less. This alternative is quickly rejected because to the overly Exogenic person, doing less is the same as being lazy, irresponsible, or quitting. Our overly Exogenic society does not respect doing less. It is viewed as weak. So the trap sends us back to trying harder. Even among highly regarded and successful leaders, the trap of pursuing Exogenic reliance becomes so hopeless that many seek medical interventions to avoid despair and depression.

The only way to build self-respect is to increase your Endogenic reliance. Building Endogenic reliance is a journey, not a quest. It is a personal discovery of who you are. You discover that every moment has the option for reflection, joy, fulfillment, openness, connection with others, creativity, or emptiness. The more you experience your Endogenic state, the more you find new and creative ways to tackle problems or find new directions. Knowing your Endogenic accomplishments leads to more self-respect, which leads to more Endogenic accomplishments. This changes the course of your life from wanting to be more like others to wanting to be more yourself.

When you apply yourself in the Endogenic state, you know when you are strong and you know how much you can rely on yourself. You encounter your inner strength and personal power and you respect yourself for what you discover.

With Endogenic strength, you have less need to measure yourself against others. Life is not limited to a never-ending race to achieve in a comparative manner. With self-respect, you have the power to innovate, inspire others, and think out of the box. Others will wish they could be more like you.

CHAPTER SIXTY-FOUR

SELLING

Endogenic confidence gives you the ability to have a strong personal connection with what you want to sell and with your audience. This connection will be real and you will feel that relationship personally

If you are tasked with making a group presentation to introduce a new product, new service, or new direction for your company, drawing from both Endogenic and Exogenic strength provides a much greater breadth of resources for communicating your ideas.

Exogenic confidence gives you the ability to analyze what needs to be communicated to your audience in order for your message to be absorbed the way you intend. For that, you need to gather material, structure your message, prepare visual rhetoric, and ensure you can deliver the information the way your audience needs it.

With Exogenic confidence, your focus is on the goal to sell or convince and it is not needed that you care about what you sell. You draw upon your training and preparation. Your mode can be upbeat and you can choose the words and body language most suited to convince others of your message. With Exogenic confidence, it is all about the end goal, the achievement, and the fulfillment of the task.

In contrast, Endogenic confidence gives you the ability to have a strong personal connection with what you want to sell and with your audience. This connection will be real and you will feel that relationship personally. If you fake it, you are not in the Endogenic state.

Endogenic confidence is fueled by your passion and belief in the product or idea; you are convinced it is of great value and you are passionate about selling it to the customer. If that is not where your confidence is coming from (and you can know by asking yourself) then you only have Exogenic confidence. With Endogenic confidence, you want the other person to understand you because you love what you are presenting to them. You want the other person to see how great it is and share the passion for the product. Instead of controlling others, you connect. The connection and the emotional experience over the product is an Endogenic experience.

By drawing upon both Endogenic and Exogenic confidence, you are using Duogenic leadership. Combining Endogenic and Exogenic is the difference between a mediocre and an outstanding presentation. Optimizing both determines the extent of your impact and propels your success. What you "sell" becomes desired. It takes experience and mindfulness to know when to engage the Endogenic state and the Exogenic state without letting one take over the other. You gain Exogenic confidence by mastering what you have learned, planned, memorized, and rehearsed. You allow for Endogenic confidence by letting go of the preparation and being in the present. With Exogenic confidence, you can rehearse until you feel you are in control. With Endogenic confidence, you can connect your message with the audience.

To unfold Endogenic strength, you must be in a calm and relaxed state in the moment of the performance. That may take Exogenic preparation too. It means knowing that you have memorized the facts that are needed and thinking through the technical aspects.

Once you have a good enough understanding of the information you need to deliver and the details needed to make it happen, you can use the power of the Endogenic state to catapult the delivery into a stellar performance. At that moment, relying on the Endogenic state goes against what you have trained for. Everyone who has experienced the fun and ease of using Endogenic power most likely discovered it by chance. With Endogenic power you are free of the "I must" and "I should" and fulfilled with the "I want." This happens when, instead of plowing through to get to the end goal, you make the moment come alive.

Having both forms of confidence means having good enough planning, good enough memorizing, less rehearsing, and less repeating. It means having presence in the moment of delivery, speaking from the essence of personal meaning, and creating a unique experience that you and your audience share.

CHAPTER SIXTY-FIVE

TRUST

*To see the difference between Endogenic and Exogenic in others lets us
see behind the curtain. It is a window through which we see what
actions, behaviors, thoughts, and feelings are motivated by*

Many people are misled because they trust someone who behaves confidently. This can be avoided by distinguishing Endogenic from Exogenic confidence.

Only Endogenic confidence is trustworthy. If you see Endogenic confidence in a person, you can rely on how that confidence appears. Endogenic confidence is based on self-reliance and it will be true to the moment and an honest reflection of the person and how that person feels. There are no cover-ups or rehearsed postures with Endogenic confidence.

On the other hand, Exogenic confidence warrants apprehension. Exogenic confidence is not reliable because it is a product of thought and a projection. Exogenic confidence can be brought to perfection and appear extremely confident. Overly Exogenic individuals who lack Endogenic confidence will look convincing and make many promises about goals and results, but will often end up disappointing others. Their performance does not deliver what their confidence promises.

How do you gauge the intention behind an action? When you think someone is trying to help you out of kindness, could it be that this person actually means to impress you or get ahead? When a colleague is sharing an interesting idea with you, could it be that this person actually means to manipulate you into something? When someone is telling you their opinion about a controversial issue at work, is that person merely telling you what you want to hear or is it the truth? When you presented an idea at a meeting, was your idea rejected because it was not right or was it because you were the one who proposed it?

There is one sure way for you to detect the intention behind an action. You can always see the difference when you are in your Endogenic state. When you are in the Endogenic state, you can recognize what state others are in. If you know that someone is in their Endogenic state, you can be certain that there is no cover-up or hidden motive in their actions. To see the difference between Endogenic and Exogenic in others lets us see behind the curtain. It is a window through which we see what actions, behaviors, thoughts, and feelings are motivated by. Our decisions are smarter when they are based on knowledge of the forces that push or draw us in a certain direction.

By knowing the difference between Endogenic and Exogenic confidence, you have an advantage not only at work, but also in your relationships with others. If Exogenic confidence triggers you to be apprehensive, you can choose to clarify or better understand what the other person really means. By making an extra attempt, sometimes you can reconnect with this person on an Endogenic level and discover truths that were hidden before.

Sometimes, however, when you look for an Endogenic connection, the other person becomes defensive and has an angry or withdrawn reaction to your engaging questions. This may be a sign that behind the Exogenic confidence there is insecurity that the person tries to hide. When that happens, a person cannot engage in a dialogue with you. The person falls back into repeating what was already said without responding to what you are asking. If you still want clarity, continue to engage. By continuing to engage in the Endogenic state, it is common to reach the heart of the other person's insecurity and communicate on a more meaningful level.

A mistake that we often make when we do not fully trust someone is to question the person in our Exogenic state. Exogenic questions come across as inquisitions and criticism. When hierarchy is involved, people may overreact to criticism and remain fixed in their Exogenic state. Their answers may sound defensive because they did not have enough Endogenic reliance to coexist with the Exogenic power they perceived in you. This frequently happens in the business world, but as a Duogenic leader, you can overcome this by switching to your Endogenic state when you detect defensiveness in others.

Chapter Sixty-Six

Uncertainty

Uncertainty allows you to continue to question and discover. It allows you to surpass the collective common opinions that all tend to be similar. It is the key to thoughtfulness and wisdom

If you have a weak Endogenic state, you cannot stand being unsure about something for long. Instead, you reach for a conclusion or opinion to end your uncertainty. This is the Exogenic state taking over, structuring, and defining. It marks the end of Endogenic learning, discovery, and openness.

One of the great strengths of the Endogenic state is the power of uncertainty. Uncertainty allows you to continue to question and discover. It allows you to surpass the collective common opinions that all tend to be similar. It is the key to thoughtfulness and wisdom.

Uncertainty requires that you observe from your Endogenic state. It takes considerable strength to observe from the Endogenic state, and beginners often make the mistake of concluding too soon. For example, you receive an email from your manager that asks for your opinion on a proposed organizational change. The proposed change is big, and you see that it would affect you in ways that are hard to predict. A few ideas come to mind about why this change would be bad, and you send off a reply.

Once a conclusion is reached, you are no longer in the Endogenic state. You easily conclude too quickly when you want to avoid a feeling that arises. It could be that you feel defensive because you fear the proposed change. Instead of actually feeling fear, you block the feeling by switching to the Exogenic state. At that moment, you have concluded something—perhaps a negative opinion or disagreement. Your conclusion may only reflect your own defense mechanism of avoiding a feeling and therefore may be suboptimal or wrong.

The gainful way to observe from the Endogenic state is to wait and not to force conclusion. The Endogenic state has the intrinsic quality that, when not disrupted, it draws to a close on itself. To draw on Endogenic reliance, you must not disrupt the cycle, which may last fractions of a second or minutes. As simple as this sounds, it may take great strength. For big decisions, you may need to revisit them in the Endogenic state over a long period of time. With practice, you learn to distinguish when the Endogenic state has ended and you are in your Exogenic state. At that point, you have the greatest possible accuracy that you are capable of for reaching a conclusion from your observation.

In a very difficult situation, allowing the feeling of ambiguity is a tremendous strength. It proves that one is ready for the situation and is open to discerning new dimensions that cannot be known. This kind of confidence keeps us alert and awake. It keeps us present in unknown situations. Only with strong Endogenic confidence can someone endure uncertainty in high-pressure situations. It gives a leader the quality of gentle, calm strength: the ability to endure highly complex and rapidly changing environments without making rash decisions; capable of holding out as long as possible before changing course because of the confidence that new ideas and new information could make a difference; knowing that a quick fix, erratic intervention, or superficial gesture only makes complex problems worse; and having the sense to know when firm direction of the Exogenic state is necessary.

Most people rely on their Exogenic confidence when the going gets tough, but this means they stop discerning and they take action too soon or too late, and with too little information. Exogenic confidence leads to wrong decisions, ineffective resolutions, stagnation, and missed opportunities.

Leaders with strong Endogenic confidence do not feel the need to hide the fact that they do not have an answer yet. They do not reject the feeling of ambiguity, because they know that their doubt and uncertainty leads to discoveries and solutions that the lack of security prompts. They know that pondering a situation and holding on to questions will lead to more intelligent answers. They know that eventually, when the moment demands, they will end their uncertainty and find the right path or speak the right words. At that moment, a great or gentle power will be exhibited. It may manifest in a profound action, charismatic speech, or insightful decision. The challenge is that such a leader may forget that others find this whole process very frightening.

The power of uncertainty is often misinterpreted as a weakness by overly Exogenic individuals. They assume a leader should never waiver. They may call it a lack of confidence. This is only because they learned it wrong. When people with weak Endogenic states think a leader does not have an answer, they feel fear and quickly lose hope that the situation can ever be resolved. They may even prefer to follow the advice of a different leader who displays Exogenic confidence instead.

Our society, with its overemphasis on the Exogenic state, teaches people, especially people in leadership roles, to not have uncertainty. Every presidential advisor earnestly tells the president that "not sure" is not an answer. People simply do not accept that from a leader. The CEO who tries to leave questions open a bit longer than the norm is quickly criticized for a lack of leadership. These reactions come from blind spots that we acquired when we learned about confidence. This learning is based on fear of uncertainty. Uncertainty is extremely threatening to people with weak Endogenic confidence.

The key to uncertainty is to have it without letting others develop fear. It might take explaining yourself to employees or perhaps just calling it your own unique style. Over time, as people see how sound your decisions are, they will begin to equate your calmness and unusual ways with accuracy, wisdom, and strength.

Special Thanks

This work would not have been possible without the generosity of special people in my life. My gratitude especially goes to my mentors Dr. Emil Grütter, Prof. Dr. Walter Herzog, and Prof. Dr. Dr. Hans Giger, without their guidance this work could not even have found a beginning; to my wonderful clients, who gave me the gift of looking through their eyes and who taught me diversity I could never have grasped on my own; to my longtime friend and colleague Dr. Esther Rosen-Bernays, who's council I rely on for wisdom; to my daughter Janice, who's empathic honesty and awareness provides me with the greatest mirror I could have wished for; and to my husband John, the most astounding and inspiring person I have ever known.

AUTHOR

Dr. Beatrice Aebi-Magee is the founder of Aebi Systems LLC, a management consulting firm providing leadership development services to CEOs, senior managers, and executives from Fortune 100 companies, technology startups, and innovative non-profit organizations. As a leadership consultant for over two decades, Dr. Aebi-Magee helps successful leaders improve their companies, advance their careers, boost strategic thinking, and become greater leaders.

A native of Switzerland, Dr. Aebi-Magee has a PhD and masters in psychology from the University of Zürich and earned the title of Psychoanalyst in association with the Freud Institute and the Psychoanalytical Institute of Zürich. She also holds an associate degree of business from KV Zürich Business School and a Swiss federal maturity certificate in Latin and modern languages. Before starting her consulting company, Dr. Aebi-Magee was an organization development project manager at Migros, one of the largest companies in Europe.

Beatrice lives in Oregon with her husband John, a two-time Inc. 500 CEO, and their daughter Janice. The lush green landscape, quiet beaches, and hiking in the Columbia Gorge and on Mount Hood are inspiring additions to her life.

www.ingramcontent.com/pod-product-compliance
Lightning Source LLC
Chambersburg PA
CBHW072119270326
41931CB00010B/1610